THE ART OF DETECTION

THE ART OF

Detection

By JACOB FISHER

New Brunswick

RUTGERS UNIVERSITY PRESS

1948

THIS BOOK is written by an investigator for investigators. During the many years actively spent as an investigator and instructor in this profession, the writer was at once impressed and perplexed by the paucity of written authorities. There are practically no basic primers or manuals available to the average investigator, especially in the field of noncriminal investigation. Even in criminal investigation, the prevailing authorities seem to emphasize the involved sciences together with their manifold technical aspects.

Investigation is one of the few professions existing today wherein most embryonic adherents are "broken in" by a more experienced investigator during a period of semi-apprenticeship. Schooling and formal training are practically unknown and exist only in a few outstanding organizations which maintain their own training institutions.

The book shelves are barren for the lay investigator. It has always been a source of wonder to the writer why tens of thousands of practicing lawyers never received the benefit of some kind of formal investigative training. Wills and probate procedure, criminal practice, real estate activity, matrimonial law, the negligence field, corporate and financial structure, collection—there is hardly a legal operation which is not closely interwoven with investigation.

Every businessman is called upon repeatedly to be a lay investigator on important matters concerning his business. As a matter of fact, there are few persons living a normal life today, no matter what the field of their endeavor may be, who are not called upon occasionally to conduct basic investigations pertaining to their own everyday activities.

A man may sublet his apartment, sell his house, pick a school for his child, consider taking out an insurance policy, survey the field for a new job, report an automobile accident, hire a maid, check up on the person courting his daughter, make a loan, trace a long vanished friend, or contemplate going into business. Today's complex civilization makes necessary numerous thoughtful investigations relating to man's normal daily endeavors. It is hoped that this volume will serve as a helpful handbook for all investigators, civil, criminal, and lay.

Grateful acknowledgment for her invaluable assistance is made to Miss Eugenia McBride of Flemington, N. J. The helpful co-operation of the following is acknowledged with thanks: Mr. Edwin G. Hundley, Superintendent of Claims, New York City office of the United States Fidelity and Guaranty Company; Mr. William Sproul Lewis, of the Industrial Credit Company, Philadelphia, Pa.; Mr. Joseph E. Henry, Manager, Allstate Insurance Company, Detroit, Michigan; Milton Berger, Esq., of the New York State Bar, New York City; A. Dudley Watson, Esq., of the New Jersey Bar, New Brunswick, N. J.; Mr. William Crawford, Manager, Hotel Century, New York City; the Honorable J. Edwin Larson, Insurance Commissioner and State Fire Marshal, Tallahassee, Florida; and Captain E. Paul Sjostrom, Supervisor, New Jersey State Bureau of Identification of the New Jersey State Police, Trenton, N. J.

JACOB FISHER

October, 1947

CONTENTS

This book is dedicated
to all persons who are engaged
in the pursuit of truth

THE ART OF DETECTION

CHAPTER ONE

WHAT IS INVESTIGATION?

AN INVESTIGATION is a search for the truth by the use and development of many arts. The investigator may employ shadowing or tailing, or he may avail himself of handwriting experts or stool pigeons. He may run down all the avenues open to him in eliminating possibilities which obscure the truth, which is the encompassing of all the facts developed by his labors.

The field of investigation is so manifold and involved that no single book can hope to do more than touch the surface of many problems presented. Volumes have been written on the complex scientific aspects of subjects like moulage, ballistics, handwriting, fingerprinting, microscopy, blood analysis, and ink analysis. The fields of criminology are so varied that they are divided into specific categories in which specially trained experts function. Thus, in a large city, there will be found police officers who investigate nothing but forgery. Others operate only on homicide cases, breaking that field down so that automobile deaths are handled by special expert investigators. Others are technicians in apprehending confidence men and still others work on juvenile cases.

Similarly, commercial investigating, as distinguished from criminal investigating, is so interwoven with the economic life of the nation that it is difficult to see how normal commercial life could function without the investigative framework upon which every enterprise is based and which is integrated into its main body.

3

In commercial work, the foremost field of investigation is in the multibillion dollar insurance business. Volumes could be written on the multifarious investigative specializations required by this industry. To name a few: automobile accidents, fires and thefts, fraudulent death claims, embezzlers' and defaulters' bonds, arson, burglary, workmen's compensations, health, property damage, casualty from many causes, and personal injury claims give but a bird's-eye view of the sweeping vista.

The great field of personnel investigation is much larger than is generally realized. There are few employees hired for any type of responsible job either by a private firm or by the government or a municipality who are not subjected to a searching investigation. The degree of the investigation and the methods employed vary with the type of work the prospective employee is to do and the amount of importance attached to the job.

The field of finance today presents investigative problems of terrific import. The entire industry of time payment, loans, installment buying, and collection is based on efficient investigation. The huge business of credit reporting is purely the sale of investigative service in a specialized field.

The special agent of a beverage company who visits soda fountains to see if his company's beverage is sold, rather than a substitute passing for the original, is an investigator. The company representative who visits barber shops to learn if his firm's hair tonic comes out of the bottle bearing his firm's label, rather than a cheaper substitute, is an investigator, albeit a specialist in his particular field. The man from the credit reporting house is an investigator.

The government employs tens of thousands of investigators, but specialization is very evident here also. A narcotic agent may spend a lifetime in the Narcotic Bureau of the Treasury Department helping to track down violators of the Narcotic

Act. In the same Department, Special Agents of the Intelligence Unit spend lifetimes perfecting the technique of catching up with income-tax violators. The Treasury Department also has operatives who are charged with apprehending counterfeiters and protecting the currency as well as the unrelated responsibility of safeguarding the life of the President. The Customs Bureau of the Treasury Department stations men in various parts of the country who are specialists in tariff laws and whose main function is to discourage smuggling. In addition, the Federal Bureau of Investigation has its own National Bank auditors, its espionage specialists, its white-slave investigators, as well as its examiners of questioned documents, fingerprint classification experts, microscopy experts, and other laboratory technicians. The Postal Service has special inspectors, and the Department of Agriculture similarly has its own investigators.

The hundreds of thousands of investigations conducted by social service agencies yearly and the great number of investigations conducted by law offices daily all leave their indelible impression on the communal life. The special problems concerning railroads, telegraph and telephone companies, and the public utilities supplying gas and electricity necessitate the service of thousands of investigators.

In the main, however, all *basic* investigative problems are alike in their method of approach. It is the purpose of this book to present so many diverse methods and aspects of investigation that it will be the rare case indeed which will not fall into one of the categories shown.

There is no "open sesame" to the mysteries of an unsolved problem. The only true common denominators are patience, common sense, and imagination with the knowledge of applying them which is born of experience. This book will reflect the cream of the experience of hundreds of investigators, gathered largely by the trial-and-error system. The reader should be saved many tedious treks through the mazes of the investigative jungle. He will be shown the short cuts and the less thorny paths that were discovered by others who traveled the same route by supplying him with the basic rules of procedure for all investigations, no matter how diverse or in what field they may occur.

The investigator should not be timid about tackling the complex cases presenting seemingly unsolvable problems. He should remember that while all human beings are different, physically and mentally, nevertheless they all were cut from the same pattern, with minor differences. Normal human brains function with the same slight degree of variation as do human limbs and other organs. There are some minds that are a bit sharper than others, in the same way that some runners or boxers or swimmers are more proficient than others competing in the same field by virtue of better training or development. One may, of course, run across an Einstein or an Edison but these instances are so few and far between in the investigative field that they can be almost entirely discounted.

Even when a matter seems abssolutely unfathomable, investigative mysteries are not too difficult to unravel when considered as problems created by another human being. One of the best means of reducing seemingly obtuse problems to a solvable level is for the investigator to place himself in the position of the subject of the investigation. What would the investigator do if he were the perpetrator of a crime and thought he was being investigated?

More often than not it will be found that the mind of the subject operates in the same channels as that of the investigator. When the investigator transposes his mind to fit the problem of the subject, he generally anticipates the moves and actions of the subject. This theory follows the premise that most minds follow similar procedure, and thoughts flow in similar channels. Because the general mold and pattern of all humans is the same, we can formulate certain rules reflecting the conduct and behavior of man. These rules can be well utilized by investigators to fit many minds and many situations.

But the investigator should also be reminded that science paradoxically shows that all humans are different. No two persons are exactly alike. Differences in blood counts, fingerprints, physiognomies, and cellular structure prove that. In the same way, no two cases are identical. There are always novel situations and problems cropping up to present a challenge to the investigator. He can never allow himself to become smug and to say, "Now I have seen it all."

One of the great fascinations of the investigative field, which acts as a magnet in keeping thousands of persons in its fold, is the continual challenge presented by the battle of wits, in which the investigator plays a vital part. He is ever in quest of the truth, and ever beset by the law violators, would-be violators, chiselers, defaulters, and connivers whom he must outwit and conquer.

There is no room for complacency in investigation. It is ever changing, and the investigator must be eternally alert and vigilant, and open-minded to new developments. But in spite of the never-ceasing novelty of methods that are uncovered, showing new and amazing efforts to avoid detection, the substance is still the same. It may vary in color or design, but it is still made of the same cloth.

It is interesting to note some examples of the "sameness" of thought in the operation of the human mind during its maneuvers to avoid detection in the commission of a crime. This also applies to "crimes of civilization" which the calculating mind evolves as distinguished from crimes of passion where more primitive reactions are displayed.

State liquor law investigators charged with eradicating illicit alcohol traffic have come across contrivances to facilitate escape or to avoid detection which are original and novel enough to be the product of a wizard's mind. Actually these gadgets were developed by backwoods people without education or criminal background. What is most interesting about these contrivances, however, is that the same or similar means were used in different parts of the country for the same purpose by persons who, when interrogated after apprehension, stated that they had developed these innovations themselves. They said that "it was just thunk out," without their ever knowing it was used by anyone else for the same purpose.

Many reports are on file concerning operators of illicit stills who attempted to escape by running across a stream that flowed along the still site. When the enforcement agents attempted to pursue them across the apparently shallow stream, they fell into deep water almost at the first step. Examination showed that the illicit distillers, apprehensive of raids, had laid planks about six inches under the surface of the water from one side of the stream to the other. The planks were invisible, but the bootleggers knew exactly where they were, and by the time the wet "revenuers" found a boat to cross the stream, the violators were well on their way toward effecting a successful escape. When these persons were finally apprehended and questioned, each one denied pirating the idea of effecting a getaway in this manner and insisted that it was his own brain child. It was not feasible for the various violators to compare notes, as the still sites covered in the reports were hundreds of miles apart and there was no indication of any contact between the persons involved.

During other raids made in wooded areas in widely scattered parts of the country, the enforcement agents kept falling flat on their faces every few steps as they approached the still. Examination showed that tiny green wires were strung about nine inches above the ground between saplings. They were invisible because of the grass, and it was almost impossible to walk more than a few paces without falling. Needless to say the operators of the still were miles away when it was finally reached. In these instances also, the operators denied ever having heard of this particular idea being used elsewhere.

In dozens of instances complete diagrams were received showing the location of illicit stills. Such sketches stated that on a certain farm there would be found a lane across a particular field which led into the woods, and that in the woods would be found the alcohol plant. The investigators would find no lane across the fields to the woods, and the woods would present a solid wall of trees. Subsequent investigation would show that there was in fact a lane, but that it had been raked and smoothed after each truck passed over it. The lane led to a seemingly solid wall of trees, but it was found that about a half dozen trees were small pines which had been sawed off elsewhere and inserted into holes in the ground. These trees were lifted out when a truck entered the woods, and replaced after the truck left the contraband area.

These actual examples show what seemingly novel and cunning methods were developed by law violators of ordinary mentality. These same procedures were in common use in different parts of the country, by various persons, each of whom thought the idea original with him.

The average charlatan, whether he seeks to outwit the police, a creditor, an insurance company, a process server, or a prospective father-in-law, is a vain person. Before he embarks on his fraudulent enterprise, he has assured himself that he has perfected a scheme to which no man can find the solution. He believes his scheme is foolproof; otherwise he probably would not attempt the swindle. His chief weakness is that he cannot quite bring himself to believe that others can be as astute as he is, and in the final reckoning that factor tends to be the cause of the downfall of all vain persons.

A smart gambler thought he had worked out a scheme of trickery that would absolutely defy detection. He spent several hundred dollars weekly making long-distance telephone calls to various race tracks. He developed a small metal container with slots in it the size of quarters, filled the slots with water, and froze it. The device was small and portable, and he used the quarter-size circles of ice to make his long-distance calls. When the coin boxes were emptied the collector didn't even have the satisfaction of picking up a few slugs. All he found for the expensive calls was water in the coin box.

At first it was believed that a contrivance had been perfected to trip the mechanism, but after a sufficient number of watered coin boxes were reported in that city, a company investigator reasoned that ice slugs had been used. The remainder of the investigation was relatively simple although quite tedious. By a very thorough and painstaking check of dry-ice sales from the distributor in that area to the ultimate consumers, it was eventually a matter of simple elimination to find a buyer who, upon being investigated, was found to be a bookmaker and better on horses—a natural user of long-distance telephone wires. A little fancy tailing apprehended the culprit.

The theory of similarity can apply to a smalltime conniver who used the same principle by freezing ice slugs the size of quarters right in his refrigerator, using the ice slugs to operate the quarter gas meter. Both were caught. Hundreds of others using the same general method have been apprehended, and each thought the idea original with him.

Most lawbreakers attach more faith to a scheme that they think is original with them. They hesitate to pirate another's method on the theory that many others, including the authorities, may know of its existence. But if the scheme is original with the trickster, in his vanity he believes his idea is known to no one else in this world. His own vanity defeats him.

This theory was never more conclusively or dramatically proved than by a series of incidents in World War II. Wars have few compensations for the pain, grief, and havoc wrought, but the millions of men and women whose lives were indentured to the military authorities provided tremendous proving grounds in many fields of endeavor, notably medicine. In the field of investigation also, certain facts were brought to light that were not only of tremendous human interest, but proved beyond a doubt, in a way that it has never been proved before, the general uniformity of human thought when it seeks to project itself into criminal channels.

During World War II, the government provided the wife of an enlisted man a family allowance of fifty dollars monthly during the time he was in the service. The family allowance went to the wife of the serviceman as a matter of legal right. The law provided that the woman had to prove that she was a lawful wife, and she had to prove nothing more. She received the allowance then as a matter of course, and the soldier husband could not stop it even if he wished to do so. This gave rise to thousands of injustices when the servicemen ascertained that their wives were living with other men or were otherwise unfaithful to them.

Even if the soldier proved his wife's infidelity, the government continued to pay the allowance to her. While it may seem like an arbitrary procedure, the army and navy contended that they would become domestic relations courts if they sought to investigate the virtues of servicemen's wives. The military authorities therefore rested on the letter of the law.

It is to be remembered that the proving ground consisted of fourteen million males, and the pickings were so good that soon lecherous females were victimizing soldiers and sailors by marrying several in order to obtain their family allowances. If it is realized that the Army alone paid out over fourteen billion dollars through its Office of Dependency Benefits, an idea can be obtained of the magnitude of this particular operation and of the involved work necessary in order to track down women plying the multiple-marriage trade.

The reports of bigamy were received thick and fast from all corners of the country by the Office of Dependency Benefits. Women who contracted five, six, and seven marriages in a few weeks were not uncommon. One woman married sixteen men in several months. As the officer in charge of all investigative activities of the Army's Office of Dependency Benefits, the writer assigned Army officers who were trained and experienced investigators to the various localities in the country from which most of the violations or suspected crimes were reported.

The reports of the investigative officers were outstandingly interesting in that, almost to a man, they reported that these unscrupulous women used the same methods in Texas as in Oregon, and the same in New York as in California. This was an entirely new field of criminology. Family allowance, as it operated in World War II, had never been known before. Yet almost in the first few months after the law went into effect, women were laying their plans to victimize the soldiers and mulct the government in every state in the Union, and the participants were city women and country women, white women and colored women, educated women and uneducated women.

The plan employed was paradoxically complex in its simplicity. A good-looking girl would frequent saloons or dances near a soldier's training center or camp. Most of these women preferred embarkation points. The average young soldier was lonely and emotionally disturbed. He would meet an attractive girl in a bar and the usual acquaintanceship would be struck up. Under the influence of a few drinks, the friendship ripened quickly. At home perhaps the soldier would not have been quite so rash or forward. His values, however, were all distorted when he was being shipped overseas. When his love-making became insistent, the girl coyly professed love for him also. She affirmed that she was a "good" girl, but she would be glad to marry the soldier. The residence requirements were generally eased up for uniformed men, and it was comparatively easy to be married almost immediately. After a few days or, in rare instances, weeks of marital life the soldier would be sent overseas.

The girl now had a marriage certificate to show that she was married to Private Rufus Jones. All she had to do to get the fifty dollars each month was to send the marriage certificate and her husband's serial number to the Army authorities. Her husband never heard from her again. She then moved to a new embarkation point and repeated the procedure, marrying someone else under another name, and so on.

After one of these women married the serviceman, she went to a nearby small-town post office and rented a box. She asked the government to send her checks to her at that box. In order not to arouse the suspicion of the postmaster, she sent herself letters to that box, using the name of her current victim. She even subscribed to magazines which were mailed to her there. From then on, it was only a routine matter to go to that town once a month to collect her mail, including the check. It was an easy matter to cash it, as she had the marriage certificate attesting to her marriage to the serviceman whose name was the same as that under which she had received her mail. When she married another serviceman, all she had to do was rent another post-office box in another town and go through the same procedure.

This wartime activity was new to the women involved. They had heard no tales about anyone else doing the same thing. They had read no stories on the subject—detective-story magazines had not included this type of crime because it was nonexistent before the war. Nevertheless each of thousands of women in every part of the United States thought up a scheme for some easy money, never dreaming that it paralleled almost exactly the illegal schemes of thousands of other women.

They were not quite so clever as they believed themselves to be, however, for over two thousand prosecutions against women were instituted in the Federal Courts for defrauding the government and servicemen on family allowance matters in World War II.

CHAPTER TWO

WHAT MAKES AN INVESTIGATOR?

LIKE every other artisan, a good investigator must be well equipped with the tools of his particular field of work. This applies equally to criminal and civil investigators.

If the investigator is a peace officer, he should have in his possession at all times his credentials and "protection" or weapons. Particular assignments may call for specific implements such as cameras, fingerprint-lifting material, disguises, or radios. Whatever they are, the peace officer should not be caught without his supplies.

The civil investigator should never be without an ample supply of paper and at least two fountain pens. It would be very embarrassing and perhaps very costly to run out of ink in the middle of an important statement if no replenishment were available.

The investigator should always carry credentials with him. The more imposing and official looking they are, the better. If the investigator is employed by a governmental or municipal organization, credentials of some form are always issued to him. Some insurance companies and credit-checking houses supply their investigators with credentials. But the vast majority of private investigators, adjusters, credit men, and welfare investigators either do not possess credentials or do not produce them if they have them.

It is important for an investigator to show his credentials when approaching a subject for interview. This in itself lends an air of dignity and importance to the interview and to the investigator. The subject more readily believes the interview a matter of some importance and not just a casual conversation, and he considers an investigator who shows impressive-looking identification as someone out of the ordinary.

If an investigator is self-employed, it would be wise for him to use a trade name for his business and then have the firm issue credentials to him, even if he is its only representative. These credentials should be as impressive looking as those issued by the Federal Bureau of Investigation. They should contain the statement that the bearer is an investigator authorized by the firm issuing the credentials to conduct investigations in its behalf. The document should contain the investigator's photograph and fingerprints on its face to lend weight to its appearance. The photograph should be kept current; if the investigator grows a mustache or dyes his hair or in any other way changes his appearance, a new photograph should be taken and new credentials issued.

When credentials are produced at the time an investigator introduces himself, they should be handed to the subject. Very often they are not read thoroughly, but the photograph is usually scrutinized carefully. Bankers and other quasi-public officials often read credentials thoroughly to determine the authority for the investigation. If the investigator tries to flash the credentials and hurriedly pockets them again, he generally arouses suspicion that there is something irregular.

A classic illustration of carelessness in producing credentials is that of a government agent who spent months trying to locate a key witness in an important conspiracy case. He finally traced the witness to the vicinity of a small town in Northern New Jersey. He called on the postmaster of the town and after identifying himself explained his mission. The postmaster said very little until the end of the interview, when the government agent hastily flapped his credentials open before the postmaster and as quickly pocketed them. This galvanized the postmaster to action. He jumped up, pointed at the agent's pocket containing the credentials, and shouted "That's him! That's the fellow you're looking for! I can lead you right to him! I always figured him as a shady character!" Although it was the investigator's own photograph, it had been taken ten years before when he was about thirty pounds lighter.

No investigator should embark upon an investigation without a thorough analysis of all the facts. He must remember that he is matching wits and pitting his mind against someone trying to outwit him. He should figuratively throw his feet up on the desk and look out of the window for a couple of hours—and think and think. He should analyze the problem presented, and he should place himself in the subject's position as much as possible in order to anticipate his moves. The groundwork for each investigation should be laid in the investigator's mind. After he embarks upon the physical investigation, it will become self-propelling, and he will then have to eliminate the new leads and clues that his investigation develops.

The investigator should at all times be careful to safeguard against loss the documents and exhibits he procures as well as those assigned to him. This is especially true when he travels very much, and he should be vigilant at all times in the protection of his papers when he is on a train, in a restaurant, bar, bus, or hotel.

In spite of the advances made by science in the field of criminology, 95 per cent of all crimes are solved by informants. An investigator is as good as the information he receives; he should have hundreds of people working for him.

The average investigator operates in a specific localized area, and it is the extraordinary case that carries him beyond the confines of his own bailiwick. In his own community an investigator should know as many persons in key observation

points as he possibly can. By that it is not necessarily meant
that he should develop people of importance. Key observation
points are used to gather facts appropriate to the particular
locality. It does not take much effort for the investigator to
develop a bootblack who has a particular stand on a certain
street corner. A dozen shines and a few friendly words with
each shine, and that corner is covered and protected for the
investigator. Someday that bootblack might become a very important witness. Waiters, maids, and private detectives in
hotels are good persons to develop without much difficulty.
When an investigator rides a bus or a trolley repeatedly, it is
not too difficult to become acquainted with the operator.
Information about criminals is not often obtained in a Sunday
school, and the investigator should not restrict his informants
to a Sunday-school class.

Few kind words are ever thrown the way of the mass of
clerks who keep the records of officialdom. A good investigator
is soon friendly with someone in each of the departments
where public records are kept. There is no such thing as idle-
ness in the life of an investigator. When he is not actually working on a case, he should be busy keeping his fences mended. It
may sometimes be necessary to "butter" some of the informants by a little gift or a lunch, but in the long run it is the
best investment an investigator can make. Contacts are the
lifeblood of the investigative profession, but they have to be
fed and nurtured, and fresh fields have to be cultivated continually.

An investigator connected with a private firm such as an
insurance company can obtain great quantities of valuable information from officials, many times in an unofficial manner.
It is of paramount importance that the private investigator be
on good terms with the police and municipal employees as
well as officials. Knowing an employee in a municipal office
quasi-socially is a great expediter in obtaining information.

Emphasis should be laid on the distinction between the words *informant* and *informer*. Roget's *Dictionary* gives as a synonym for *informer* the word "squealer." *Informant* is defined as a "reporter" or "spokesman." There is a world of difference between the two words. After a year or so spent in cultivating informants, the good investigator should be able to sit at his desk and obtain his major leads over the telephone from people he knows in every walk of community life.

No good investigator should ever overlook the opportunity of becoming acquainted with a train companion, telegraph messenger, mail carrier, waiter, cab driver, theater usher, or grocery clerk. He should record their names and addresses for future development and reference. At the original time of cultivating acquaintance, there is no absolute necessity for the investigator to disclose his business. The alert, inquisitive investigator soon develops a sixth sense about a person who can be of future use to him, and he develops that person accordingly.

When the investigator interviews a subject at his home or office, he should seek to promote a common ground for conversation and develop a mutual plane of interest. This is especially important when the witness to be interviewed is absolutely disinterested personally, yet can supply information that can be of great help to the development of the case. If the investigator sees a picture of the subject apparently taken on a fishing or hunting trip, this would provide safe ground for discussion in order to arouse the interest of the witness as well as liking for the interrogater. If there should be nothing in the room to indicate an activity or hobby of the subject, a comment about a photograph, possibly that of a wife or child, might serve as an opening. If there are no openings such as the ones suggested, the investigator might comment on the fine appearance of the room or the furniture. The point is that anything that tends to personalize this part of the interview will be of help in breaking down the barriers. The investigator should avoid any political or religious discussion unless something in the room or on the person of the subject indicates what his leanings may be.

The investigator should learn to recognize fraternal emblems, Phi Beta Kappa keys, and school and fraternity badges. He should recognize military service emblems and lapel buttons in order to make proper comment to the wearer of the insignia. The subject will be pleased to have the emblems or insignia noticed, and they may provide a perfect opening wedge for a satisfactory interview. If by chance the investigator should be a member of the same organization as the subject, this should be used as a bond.

While on duty no investigator should ever wear a fraternal emblem that might antagonize a subject. If an investigator happens to be a Mason, a member of the Knights of Columbus, or any other organization, he should not wear his insignia when approaching an unknown subject. If he ascertains by general conversation that his subject and he are both members of the same organization, he can then identify himself if the circumstances warrant. It is surprising how many witnesses have proved non-co-operative toward an investigator because of his lodge insignia.

Many thousands of trials and lawsuits have been decided, not on the equities and facts submitted to the jury, but on the personalities of the litigants and the lawyers involved. A lawyer frequently wins or loses a case because of the friendship or animosity shown to him by the jury rather than on the merits of the case. Whether the investigator is personally liked by the witness will in many cases determine the degree of information obtained.

The appearance of an investigator is important. A seasoned investigator blends with the background. He is unobtrusive and never loud in dress or manner. The best investigators in the country are not prototypes of the movie G-men. The handsome, swashbuckling private detective with the slouch hat is a product of the detective thrillers.

Whenever an investigator obtains information, he must always remember that he may be called upon to testify in court about the facts he has obtained. He should carry a diary of his activities at all times. The time and place of each interview should be noted as well as information relative to the persons interviewed and a résumé of events. The entries in the diary should be made concurrently with the event or immediately thereafter. This diary is the investigator's Bible. He should never be without it. When he is on the stand in a court testifying he may refer to it to refresh his memory. It not only serves to recall points involved, but also impresses the jury with the fact that the investigator is a careful and methodical man who refers to his records for accurate testimony.

When testifying, the investigator should be quiet and dignified. He should not argue with the attorneys, and he should answer responsively the questions put to him. He should not volunteer any information. His appearance should be neat and unobtrusive, because to a large extent the jury will judge his testimony by its impression of him. Little things sometimes leave lasting impressions. When an investigator is on the stand he generally sits there with his legs crossed. Nine male witnesses out of ten do the same. If the investigator wears no garters and his socks dangle on his shoe tops, he presents a rather slovenly appearance.

The investigator's diary should be complete and honest. When giving testimony on a witness stand, the investigator should not peer at his diary to impress the jury and then improvise a story that does not appear in it. This is dangerous, and more than one investigator who tried it was caught in a very embarrassing position, for the attorneys have a right to see the diary from which the recollections are obtained. If the facts in the diary are at variance with the testimony, the investigator's case becomes quite hopeless.

The diary is extremely important for many other reasons. It presents a complete history of the activities of the investigator. If there is any administrative question raised about the investigator's expense account or travels, or time spent on a case, the diary provides the best evidence. Far more important, however, is the fact that the diary presents the best insurance to the investigator against being "framed" or trapped. These are situations of which a good investigator must always be aware, and while they may not occur often eternal vigilance is imperative.

A diary record once saved a government investigator's career. During the prohibition era it was common practice for the government agents to install wire supervisions or, as more commonly called, wire taps on the telephones of suspected smugglers and illicit distillers of alcohol. The supervisor or wire tapper was a government agent who took the recordings of every conversation, and if any talk was significant he would report it to headquarters immediately so that proper action, either in the form of a raid or arrest, could be taken. The supervisor manipulated a rheostat control to cut in very gradually and gently, so that there would be no sudden fading or diminution of current, which would cause a rapid fading of the voice and warn the suspect that there was some interference on his telephone.

A wire tap was placed on the telephone of a well-known suspected racketeer. For several weeks the wire was cold and uninteresting, but several guarded conversations indicated that the government was on the right track. Then a "hot" conversation broke one night between the suspect in New York and a henchman in Philadelphia. The boss asked his henchman if the boatload of whiskey landed at Brigantine Island, New Jersey, on August 3 was disposed of. The conversation took place on August 29. The Philadelphia voice said the liquor was all sold and he would bring the money in.

"I had to pay Joe Brady five thousand dollars the night the load arrived, however," the Philadelphia henchman said. "He was at Atlantic City that day," he continued, "and knew about our boat. He told me he would knock the load off if it landed —unless I came across. I paid him the five G's and thought it cheap."

Joe Brady (the name used here is fictitious) was an ace government agent whose integrity had been thought beyond reproach and who was a thorn in the side of this particular gang. Although the speakers were criminals, many a man has been condemned on less evidence. He was called in and asked to show his diary. It was posted to date. On August 3 he was not even in New Jersey. Every one of the persons he had interviewed that day had been in New York City; they were questioned, and the diary was substantiated in its entirety.

A member of the Philadelphia gang who subsequently testified for the government stated that Joe Brady was so hated by the mob they were determined to remove him from the area in which he operated. It was thought that the easiest way to do it was to blacken his reputation even if they couldn't actually make a bribery-acceptance charge stick. When their boss from New York visited them one day, he jokingly remarked that he knew his wire was tapped, as some novice was doing the tapping job in such an amateurish fashion he was tempted to tell him so over the phone. The Philadelphian, however, saw a golden opportunity to frame Brady by engaging in a fraudulent conversation about him on the tapped wire, knowing that the conversation would be taken down and reported immediately. It almost succeeded—except for Brady's diary.

The investigator should be discreet when he interviews women alone in their homes. If he knows in advance that he must interview a woman who lives in a furnished bedroom or a hotel room, he should arrange to have another investigator or a colleague present. Because of the nature of the work, many persons of dubious reputation have to be contacted by investigators, often in questionable surroundings. While Joe Brady was lucky, it is best to avoid any accusations that might reflect on an investigator's conduct. All too many times, an accusation against an investigator is unfortunately tantamount in the eyes of the public to a conviction. Incidentally, whenever an investigator enters a questionable place for an interview, he should try to sit on a plain chair and avoid overstuffed chairs, couches, or sofas. This is suggested not from a moral standpoint, but to insure the investigator against leaving with a mess of lice or bedbugs in addition to his statement.

The good investigator should develop a reputation for squareness. It is axiomatic that he is expected to be honest, but he should use discretion to make his honesty and integrity outstanding in the community. He should meet all his commitments, and above all, he should protect his informants. If the information he receives is of such a nature that the informant requests that the source not be disclosed, the investigator should never fail to respect this request, regardless of any pressure or inducements offered to him. An investigator is often the confidant and repository for family secrets, and he should never gossip about what he knows.

The good investigator should realize that no case is important enough to justify framing any person. It is understandable that there are times when a case can become so exasperating, or a particular suspect so irritating that the urge to manufacture false testimony becomes very great. Regardless of the moral aspects, no investigator should risk his reputation and that of his company by ever engaging in such practices. No case is worth it, and there are too many legitimate means by which information can be obtained.

There is a racketeer in an Eastern city who for the past ten years has had all his pockets sewed up as soon as he bought a suit except the watch pocket. This little pocket serves for whatever money he carries with him. He is mixed up in a dozen illegal enterprises, but the authorities as yet have been unable to prove his actual connection with any of them. He has been arrested only once in his life—about ten years ago—for carrying a concealed weapon. For that offense he served one year in jail. He vehemently avers to this day he never carried a gun in his life and that no policeman is ever going to plant one on him again.

It is a reflection on our entire police system and definitely does not pay in the end for police or private investigators to employ similar tactics. Many investigators sometimes let their own enthusiasm carry them away, and often a situation becomes colored or a false solution is forced. Then it becomes difficult to find the original color or actual facts.

While enthusiasm and initiative in investigation are cardinal virtues, no investigator should start an investigation with the thought that he must obtain only a certain type of solution. If he does so, he is too often inclined to bend and twist facts to obtain the desired solution. He is tragically wrong, for a twisted fact is like twisted metal—much weaker than before.

The investigator should not become officious or overbearing in his attitude. Many develop what is variously called a "cop complex," "copitis," or "agentitis." The easiest way for an investigator to be shunned by his brother investigator is to develop such a manner.

The investigator should remember that he has a certain standing in the community. How high he goes and how much he is respected depends on himself. A good investigator, unless he works for a salary for a company, or unless he has contracted to work on a per hour or per diem basis, should not hesitate to charge fees commensurate with the results obtained. In too many cases the painstaking tedium of a detailed investigation is not known to the principal retaining him. The trained investigator should consider himself a professional man, and when he performs a particularly brilliant piece of work, he should charge accordingly if the principal is in a position to pay.

A famous will case which was recently decided in New York gives proof of the point. An elderly spinster died leaving many millions of dollars. Several hundred persons filed claims contending that they were relatives of the deceased. One man based his case on an old Bible containing certain entries allegedly in the handwriting of the spinster's deceased brother, purportedly made at the time the claimant was born out of wedlock, and stating that the spinster's brother was the father of the claimant. Experts declared the handwriting to be that of the old lady's brother, and the claimant was declared to be her nephew.

The executors of the estate retained a private firm to continue the investigation. About a year later the case was reopened. After a trip to Europe, where lumber firms and paper mills were thoroughly checked, the private investigators brought back proof to show that the Bible introduced as evidence was not printed until many years after the purported entry at the time of the claimant's birth. The entries were proved to be forgeries, and the "nephew" was sent to Sing Sing. A fee reported to be several hundred thousand dollars was well earned for the results obtained.

The good investigator will never act in a superior manner toward any person when seeking to obtain information, and he must remember there is a certain respect that must be accorded those who by their position in life expect special recognition. If this recognition is not forthcoming, the information the investigator desires may likewise not be forthcoming. It is not advocated that the investigator be unctuous or humble, but he must develop a sense of human values and apply them to the persons he contacts. It is apparent that the approach to the bank president is rather different from the approach to the bootblack. The degrees of difference are worked out by the investigator who bases the distinctions on the human elements involved.

It does not always follow that a person of means or one in a position of accepted importance is the only one to receive special recognition. The theory of relativity applies to all phases of human relations. For example, if the investigator is to interview an elevator starter, he may think it is just another interview of a person engaged in work that isn't generally considered to be executive. But an elevator starter in action is an executive; he is the top man to a group of elevator operators. He is their boss, the man who picks those who work nights and Sundays. He is the man who recommends a raise. He is the man who gives the newly painted car with the good brakes to his favorite. The operator whom the starter dislikes gets the old car with the slipping cables, the dripping grease, and no electric fan. It can be seen, therefore, that when a starter is interviewed in front of his men, he is to be accorded the respect due him.

The investigator is always delving into the complexities of the human mind. This is as true before he starts on any actual duties as it is after he begins operating on an assignment. The art of cultivating informants is really a fine study in psychology. The investigator should evaluate thoroughly the informants he seeks to develop. Persons voluntarily give information for many reasons. There are some imbued with the "cops and robbers" complex, and they get a thrill out of working with the law or with an investigator. It makes them feel important and gives them the feeling of participating in something adventurous themselves. There are others who will volunteer information about shady characters because they are simple, honest citizens doing what they believe to be their civic duty. Another group frankly pass out information to those who butter them thickest.

Still another group will be good sources of information because the subject of the complaint is a business competitor. Others will give the investigator information he seeks merely because he has cultivated them, and they consider him a friend.

There are many other motivating factors, and the investigator should study them in connection with the informants so that he can utilize their knowledge to the best advantage.

CHAPTER THREE

FINDING THE WITNESS

ONE of the saddest spectacles of the science of investigation is the investigator who fails to use the available public sources of information. It could not be that he simply does not care to tap existing official sources. He just does not know of the existence and functions of numerous bureaus which can be of inestimable aid. It is heartbreaking to see an investigator plodding along painfully day after day to locate an important witness when a telephone call to a proper agency might supply the needed information forthwith.

The investigator's task is to find those persons who know the answer to moot questions and then to obtain from them in understandable and comprehensive form the germane information. Finding a witness or interested party is the foundation of the investigation. Without witnesses there can be no trial or no determination or adjudication of the facts. The witness is the cornerstone upon which the entire investigative proceeding rests.

The percentage of witnesses who cannot be found if enough effort is exerted is infinitesimal. A famous insurance investigator once said that the man who could not be found is the man at the bottom of the sea and even then he must be at the bottom at its point of greatest depth.

Anyone alive can be found if enough effort is put forth. The investigator's good judgment about the importance of the case, however, and the importance of the missing witness in the case, should determine how much effort shall be expended. It is apparent that it is much easier to pay a claim of five hundred dollars when it would cost one thousand dollars to find the only person who could possibly defeat the claimant's demand.

When the investigator conducts his preliminary analysis of a case, prior to making any personal contact with the witnesses, one important step for special consideration is the list of known witnesses set forth according to type. Thus each interested witness who has something to gain, or whose friends or relatives may profit or be protected by the investigation and the incidental actions and recommendations of the investigator, should be placed in one category of friendly or co-operative witnesses. In this category may also be placed the voluntary informants, including jealous neighbors and business competitors, disgruntled sweethearts, other investigative and enforcement agents, and civic-minded citizens who wish to report irregular occurrences. The voluntary informants comprising this group have not been cultivated or developed by the investigator and may be unknown to him. Complaints emanating from the voluntary informants are commonly called "reported violations."

The second class of interested witnesses comprise those who stand to lose something from the investigation. In this category are included fugitives and their families, suspected violators, debtors, defaulters, and concealers.

The third and last class of witnesses includes those who are disinterested personally in the issues involved but who are in possession of facts that may lead to a solution of certain disputed or unknown points. This class has nothing to gain or lose by the results of the investigation and is generally the most reliable of all the groups because no personal motivation exists. A person in this group may sometimes have the desired information thrust upon him by a combination of circumstances, such as being a witness to an accident or a murder. Or he just may be in possession of facts which the investigator needs; the custodian of pertinent records and a person possessing knowledge of another's reputation are examples.

The expert's testimony is ordinarily considered to fall into the last category, that of the entirely disinterested witness. But many observers favor the belief that the expert who testifies on behalf of a particular litigant or interested party to prove handwriting, physical condition, or any other fact should be placed in the first category the same as any witness who favors a particular person or cause.

After the witnesses have been classified by types, the investigator should question all the friendly witnesses first. The basic reason is that he can obtain all their available information without undue effort. The investigator will have a complete picture of all the facts they can give. Perhaps it will be a one-sided picture, subject to modification later, but he will have at his disposal information that may subsequently enable him to dispute or refute the allegations advanced by the unfriendly witness. If this procedure were not followed the investigator would ordinarily have no means of knowing whether or not the unfriendly witness were lying.

The friendly witness is eager to meet the investigator and to tell him all he knows, for he believes himself to be on the same team. The investigator should have no difficulty in arranging appointments with the witnesses in this class by merely writing to them and suggesting the time and place for an interview. The witness will in most cases be at the designated place to meet the investigator, who can plan his day's work without losing time on witnesses who are not at home if he goes there without prearrangement. The investigator can confirm the appointment by enclosing a short appointment slip in his letter requesting that the witness return it in a self-addressed stamped envelope. There is practically no difficulty at all in meeting the co-operative witness provided his whereabouts is known; but the investigator who goes out without previously notifying this type of witness that he will come is a very wasteful man indeed, for he is throwing away his most precious commodity—time.

In most cases the friendly witness will know about the pending investigation, and no detailed explanation need be made in the appointment letter. There are sometimes instances, however, where a witness may not know that he may stand to gain by the investigation, or he may not know at all that he is an interested party. For these reasons he will not generally go out of his way to facilitate matters for the investigator. An example of such a witness is a missing heir or legatee in a probate proceeding. In such cases it is well to state briefly in the letter that the appointment sought is in reference to some money or property that may be due the witness. He will then usually be at the appointed place, with the letter in his outstretched hand, palm up.

Many investigators have stretched this type of statement in a letter rather unscrupulously, using this approach as bait for the witness even in cases when the witness was absolutely disinterested. These rash statements without foundation are not advocated, because if the witness realizes that he has been baited, the danger is great that he will disavow the statement he gives the investigator if the matter comes up at trial.

It is wise never to notify the hostile witness that the investigator will call upon him. If informed of an impending call, the witness in this group may deliberately absent himself from home or, if he receives the investigator there, he may have a story concocted in anticipation of the investigator's visit. This story may be far removed from the truth and be submitted in an attempt to mislead. The element of surprise in confronting the unfriendly witness cannot be too strongly emphasized. If surprised, the witness may tell a great deal more when first questioned than he will after he has a few days' time to consider the matter, with possible reinforcement and suggestions from friends and lawyers. It is best when feasible to interview a hostile witness away from friends or family. A place of employment is ideal for this purpose. When an unfriendly witness is bolstered by the presence of a friend or relative, he is more inclined to be recalcitrant or evasive, and if he refuses to talk at all, the refusal takes on added firmness.

When the investigator calls at the place of employment of the witness and identifies himself to the personnel officer or employer, the witness will generally be produced. In addition to the fact that the conditions under which the interview will be conducted will be fairly comfortable, since an office or desk is generally supplied, the witness is placed at a disadvantage psychologically. He is at his place of employment and probably does not want his employer to know that he is involved in any questionable proceedings, which inference many persons draw from an investigator's interview. The setting is greatly to the advantage of the investigator. The witness is caught by surprise. He is uncomfortable because he does not have the supporting bulwark of the presence of members of his family. He is more uncomfortable because he is the center of attention at the place where he earns his livelihood, and the longer he stays away from his work, the more he will be spotlighted. The general tendency of the witness therefore is to tell all, to get it over with quickly without taking time to concoct a story, to be evasive, or to parry and thrust with the investigator. The witness wants to get back to his work quickly and without ado. In endeavoring to reach a witness at a factory of any size, it will expedite matters greatly and possibly save a long wait if the investigator has available the exact department or division in which the employee works.

The investigator should unhesitatingly use his telephone. It is his cheapest investment. While he should not question principal witnesses by telephone except for appointments, he should use this convenience unstintingly on incidental witnesses to collateral issues such as determining the place of business of a principal witness. He does not have to disclose the reason for seeing the witness, nor does he have to disclose any of the facts of the case to the incidental witnesses. After conducting the incidental investigation by locating the place of employment of the witness, he will return to the main channel by a personal interview.

In using the available telephone facilities, the investigator should identify himself and his organization when requesting the desired information, stating that it is needed "in furtherance of an investigation being conducted by my organization." Often the incidental witness, who may be a clerk in a public office or another investigative agency, or a local business man or banker, may say, "How do I know you are Mr. Wilkins of the Garden State Investigative Agency? Perhaps you are a creditor, or you are involved in a domestic tangle with the witness."

The answer to that query, which is made very frequently, is for the investigator to instruct the witness to call him back. At the same time, the witness should be advised of the page number in the telephone book containing the listing and number of the investigator's office. This procedure will prove the authenticity of the given telephone number and the caller.

It is extremely surprising how many firms will not give out information concerning an employee to individual persons. As soon as an investigative agency is retained to procure the same information, however, it is usually made available immediately.

The third class of witness, comprised in the disinterested group, may be interviewed at any time without appointment if he is a part of officialdom. It is generally wise to approach the nonofficial witness without previous notification even though some waiting may result. The reason for this is that the absolutely disinterested person may resent being told to be at a designated place at a certain time without being consulted as to his wishes in the matter. It may also cause him to stay away at the specified time if he is a type that is wary of courts or subpoenas or of being annoyed and harassed by investigators on matters that do not concern him. An appointment letter may dignify the visit with importance and possible future involvements, but if the investigator makes the visit without advance notice, the witness may spontaneously give the necessary information.

The greatest challenge in the field of investigation is the painstaking efforts that are seemingly vainly expended in an endeavor to locate a person who has apparently vanished. Taking up the challenge is often a necessity if the investigator is to maintain his equilibrium and confidence. If he treats some of these complex matters as a personal challenge to his acumen, he will get as much pleasure in unraveling the machinations of cunning and conniving minds as he would in winning a poker or bridge game.

The investigator should learn to conserve his energy in locating a missing witness by first using those facilities available to him that are closest to hand. As step after step fails, he should then branch out to embrace other and more involved instrumentalities. For instance, if an investigator calls at the last known address of a potentially important witness and finds a vacant apartment, he should not seek any other known sources of information until he has exhausted whatever information is available at the premises he is visiting. He may interview neighbors or the superintendent of the apartment house. He may find his answer right there at the last known address, thus eliminating the necessity of time-consuming visits to other sources.

If no one in the neighborhood can enlighten him offhand, the investigator should ask the superintendent or janitor for the name of the truckman who moved the tenant while he can obtain it without much effort. Practically all apartment houses keep records of truckmen coming on the premises in case of damage to the premises inflicted by "moving men." The investigator should note the name for future reference, but it does not necessarily mean that he should look up the truckman immediately. There may be an easier, more accessible source of information. In the case of separate dwellings the realty agent may be able to supply similar information.

Other valuable information can be obtained from the landlord or from the realty agent if either is found on the premises. The investigator is to assume that he does not know how much effort he will have to expend in finding the witness, and it is therefore wise for him to engage himself in gathering all clues available at a given place so that he does not have to backtrack. If there is a lease, the investigator will generally find in its supporting papers the name of the employer of the witness, together with the names of several references. It is readily apparent how valuable this information may be. The invesigator should always ascertain if the witness has children and, if so, their approximate ages.

At this point the reader may be thinking "Why doesn't the investigator go to the post office to see if there is a change of address filed?" That may be the next step, but the current task of the investigator is to eliminate all available clues at the place he is now visiting. He may not have to visit the post office.

If, however, the investigator does visit it, this is a case where a pre-established liaison with a postal inspector will often prove helpful. When information of this kind is needed the postal inspector can obtain it quite easily with little expenditure of time. Thus when a personal contact has been established, a telephone call to him will generally produce the desired information if it is a matter of record. The average postmaster or substation superintendent will disclose no information of this kind over the telephone to a person unknown to him, and a personal visit would then be necessary. If a witness seeks to avoid creditors, or has been involved in a scandal, or is avoiding the investigator, there probably would not be a change of address on file in the post office.

Up to this point, even if there is no change of address on file, the investigator should ordinarily have a large portfolio of information collected about the potential witness. If it is found the witness has children of school age, their current school should be ascertained, and either a visit to the school or a telephone call to the Board of Education should elicit their present address because it is mandatory that they have a transfer from one school to another showing credits earned. If there was a lease, the references given therein may be questioned, or the employer of the tenant as shown on the lease may be a source for information.

Another simple yet almost infallible source of information is the local electric and gas company, advocated as the best short cut of all. All subscribers for gas and electricty in an urban community must transfer their accounts if they move within the same town. A telephone call to the utility company will usually produce the new address. It is to be remembered that these calls are not just made to the company in the abstract. It is presumed the investigator has made his contacts in the communtiy and met the proper official in the utility company personally so that all calls for this type of information may be made to him.

This source goes even further. If the witness has moved out

of town and has not transferred his account, there still is a strong possibility of obtaining the current address. Most utility companies supplying gas or electricity provide that customers make a deposit when an account is opened. If a customer moves out of town and closes his account, he will usually write to the company requesting the return of his deposit. Specific inquiry must be made by the company on this point, and if the deposit was returned, the investigator will be able to obtain the address to which the return was made.

If all of the above sources of information have been tapped and have failed to produce the desired information, the investigator might next communicate with the Motor Vehicle Bureau of that state. Most state laws provide that a licensed driver or owner of a motor vehicle must file notice of his change of address or be subject to penalty. The Motor Vehicle Bureau is of invaluable aid in rural districts where most persons almost of necessity use automobiles.

Another source to be tapped is the Commissioner or Board of Elections. All voters are registered by wards or election districts. If a voter moves from one election district to another, provision is generally made that a record be kept of the transfer. These records are public, as are most official records.

The records of the 1940 Census have proved to be of invaluable assistance in locating persons. Furthermore statements made to a census taker at a time when they obviously were not self-serving are of great assistance in proving other points in issue, as for example the status of an alleged common-law marriage or the paternity of a child. Election records, school records, rental records, and census records are all great aids in shedding light on the history of persons.

An outgrowth of World War II was the Selective Service System. Complete dossiers on all registered men between the ages of 18 and 65 are on file, together with employment and skill tabulations as set forth by the registrants themselves. Changes of address were also required to be filed with local boards.

The Bureau which has the largest number of active files in its archives is the Social Security Board, the head office of which is located in Baltimore, Maryland. Those agencies entitled to receive information from this Board have a veritable bonanza. The current employer, that is the employer for the last quarter of the year, of every possessor of a Social Security Number files a report with the Board for the period.

In tracing a person, the investigator should pick up all information as to abnormalities or other outstanding physical characteristics. The alertness of one process server and the fact that he remembered a personal characteristic of the person sought enabled him to serve a summons in a million-dollar action.

The defendant successfully defied service of the legal papers for many months and he was able to continue milking a corporation. No photograph of the subject was available. One of the known characteristics of the defendant was that he was left-handed. One evening a person interested in effecting service on the schemer called up the process server and told him that the man he wanted could be found at a stage-side table at a certain night club.

The process server went to the club immediately and surreptitiously asked the headwaiter where Mr. X was sitting. The headwaiter said he knew of no such man. The orchestra was playing at the time, and most of the guests at the tables near the stage were dancing. The process server quickly went over to the vacant tables and looked at each one, hoping to find a clue to the one used by the defendant. On one table his keen eyes detected a paper folder of matches half used. The empty spaces where matches had been removed, however, were on the left side of the folder, indicating that a left-handed person had removed the matches from left to right instead of from right to left as a right-handed person would ordinarily do. When the occupant of that chair returned, the process server immediately confronted him with the summons without asking him if he were Mr. X. The flabbergasted defendant did not take the trouble to deny his identity, but mumbled something about seeing his lawyer.

While the subject of process servers is being mentioned, it might be well to comment on novel means used to gain access to a defendant for the purpose of serving him. While the incident itself is interesting, the significance of the use of initiative and imagination as shown in the current instance cannot be overlooked.

The obstinate defendant lived in a house in a small town. He defied service and holed himself up on his property, which was surrounded by a large white fence. The process server became especially exasperated because the subject for service would sun himself in the back yard daily. The reason service could not be effected was that a large and savage male police dog roamed the yard, snarling at anyone who even came near the fence, and he was definitely ready, willing, and able to bite.

One bright morning the process server jauntily unlatched the gate and walked through the yard toward the dumfounded defendant sitting on his easy chair. The savage dog fawned at the feet of the process server, licked his shoes, and squealed with delight. Service was effected, and the process server said later that it was worth a thousand dollars in satisfaction to him to pull the stunt.

For some time the server refused to tell how he won over the dog, but the truth came out eventually, as the secret was too good to keep. The process server had a female dog. Once, when she was in heat, he procured some urine from his bitch and soaked some swabs of ordinary cotton in the liquid. He then placed several of the wads of cotton in his trouser cuffs, and when he approached the male dog, the old pooch was his best pal. The server admitted, however, that he had tested his formula the day before the service was actually made, with the fence between himself and the dog. That day the dog dashed toward the fence, but when he approached within smelling distance, the dog's growl changed to a whine, his bristles subsided, his tail wagged, and he had all the ear-marks of greeting an old friend—or sweetheart.

It is not necessary for the investigator to use all the methods suggested. Likening the situation to that of a hitchhiker, although many cars represent a potential ride, only one is necessary to get him to his destination. Only one of the means indicated may be the vehicle to locate the witness or apprehend the fugitive.

If the subject to be located is a criminal or has a criminal record, the various crime indices in the major police departments can be checked, because the methods used by different criminals are indexed. This avenue of investigation is of special importance when the investigator suspects that the name of the subject he seeks to find may be an alias.

If the investigator suspects that the witness is an alien, or has been an alien, the Immigration Bureau may be in a position to supply leads from its lists of registered aliens. If this Bureau is consulted it is well to know that steamship lines must file a complete list of passengers and crews. Air lines also keep passenger lists. If an alien has been naturalized, the law requires that as a condition precedent to becoming a citizen he must produce witnesses to his good character who have known him for a specified number of years. These witnesses may prove instrumental in locating him.

A missing witness who is deliberately hiding out is often

found through the medium of his bank if that is known. A perusal of the current checks cashed will readily show the present whereabouts of the subject.

If it is known that a subject owns some real property, a check with the assessment lists will show to what address the tax bills are sent.

About fifteen million men and women served in the last war. The Veterans' Bureau, the demobilization records of the Army, Navy, Marine Corps, and Coast Guard can be of tremendous assistance in locating a person who is a veteran.

Alphonse Bertillon, of the Paris Police Department, is generally credited with having developed the first practical identification system by the use of the portrait parlé, which consists of a clear and precise method of describing a person and also uses photography. The theory behind this system is based on the fact that the human skeleton is unchangeable after the twentieth year and the fact that it is impossible to find two human beings with identical bone structure. Exact instrumental measurements of the ears, head, feet, fingers, toes, arms, and nose are made. Coupled with these are other characteristics such as color of eyes and hair, scars, height, tattoos, posture, and individual peculiarities.

The ears, specifically, are examined for many characteristics the basic patterns of which remain unchanged from birth until death. Regardless of the natural growth of the ear, the principal parts, consisting of the helix, the lobule, the tragus, the antitragus, the antihelix, and the concha remain unchanged in shape, form, and inherent peculiarities.

Although the portrait parlé system is still used in some European cities, in many places it has given way to the fingerprint system of identification. Although fingerprinting was not adopted until 1901 by Scotland Yard, which was the first modern police agency to use this means of identification, there is evidence that even before Christ the Chinese used fingerprints as seals for personal identification. The Tang dynasty, which flourished in China over one thousand years ago, used a fingerprint system of identification based on loops and whorls, which is the basis of our present system used almost universally. The Babylonians also pressed their fingerprints into soft clay to record important transactions.

It is difficult to estimate how many people in the United States, now living, have been fingerprinted. Various authorities place the figure at fifty to sixty million persons. When one realizes that, in addition to the millions of criminals whose fingerprints are on record, government employees, members of the armed forces, defense and security workers, aliens, various state and municipal employees, and others must also be fingerprinted, an idea may be formed of this tremendous source of information. Actually, more than 100 million fingerprints are on file with the Federal Bureau of Investigation. This figure includes persons in foreign countries and many now dead.

Every state in the Union has some form of central State Identification Bureau generally related to the State Police. The respective state headquarters receive prints from the various police agencies in their jurisdiction. This central agency has competent experts and facilities for lifting, photographing, or developing latent fingerprints. Indexes of fingerprints, names, aliases, photographs, and methods of crime are usually kept. The investigator would be wise to use his own state identification bureau liberally.

The all-embracing and largest agency containing fingerprint records, however, is the Federal Bureau of Investigation of the United States Department of Justice. All law enforcement agencies in the land, as well as the military, governmental, and municipal authorities ordinarily send to this Bureau copies of each set of fingerprints taken.

An investigator seeking to locate a missing person should

never overlook writing to the Director of the Federal Bureau of Investigation, Washington, D. C., to request a fingerprint record. The return may be great for the small amount of time expended in writing. The investigator should not, however, restrict his efforts to the Bureau in Washington. If he is conducting an intensive investigation, he should never fail to check with the local authorities, because the subject might have been arrested for a misdemeanor or nominal offense, one not necessitating the taking of fingerprints. A record of the arrest, however, would be present locally. In certain states, if a defendant is tried and acquitted, he may request the return of his fingerprints. Even in states where this procedure is permitted, however, the local police archives will have a complete record of the arrest and the facts leading up to it, all of which may prove of assistance to the investigator.

The United States Post Office system presents a method of helping to locate persons that is unique and efficacious. In investigation parlance this is called "the mail cover." The average investigator or law enforcement agency cannot obtain authority to have a letter opened, which is forbidden by law except in certain instances prescribed by regulation, such as the right of a censor to open mail. Assume that the investigator knows the address of the wife or other relatives of the subject, and that constant surveillance of the place brought negative results. The investigator feels strongly, nevertheless, that the subject sends mail to the person or persons at this address.

The investigator requests the post-office inspector serving the particular area to place a "mail cover" on the premises occupied by the relatives of the missing witness. The post-office inspector in turn requests the superintendent of the post-office branch serving the area including the given address to observe the "mail cover" routine. The superintendent then holds out all mail for this address for just a few minutes, places a piece of transparent tissue paper over the front of the envelope, and traces all markings showing through. He repeats the process for the rear side of the envelope. This same procedure is followed for every piece of mail sent to the given address. The tissue copy will include the postmark showing the mailing place, the return address if shown on the original envelope, and any other markings included thereon. The original mail is given immediately to the mail carrier for delivery, and the tracings are sent to the post office inspector, who in turn forwards them to the investigator. A "mail cover" is generally placed for a period of fifteen or thirty days.

After the original arrangements are made, the investigator need do nothing further in the matter except to receive and analyze the tissue-paper tracings received promptly from the postal inspector. Incidentally, no one but the postal inspector knows where the request for the "mail cover" originated and why it is in operation.

If the missing witness has placed his return address on an envelope, the investigator has something tangible to proceed with. If there is no return address, the handwriting may be of help. If in this case the handwriting does not help, or the writing is all typewritten, a series of letters coming from a particular point may merit investigation at the point of mailing. It is especially significant when several letters come from a particular post office but bear no return address. Such letters are rarely business letters and would be worth investigation.

This method of working through the office of the post-office inspector is a tremendous timesaver for the investigator, as such an office usually covers a whole state or in some cases several states. After the original request by the investigator to the post-office inspector, all subsequent requests relative to the "mail cover" go to the various postmasters or superintendents from the inspector, and the investigator has only to await results.

A converse method of obtaining information pertaining to a missing witness or fugitive may be obtained by way of the postal service. Assume the "mail cover" fails to give the desired information, yet the investigator feels absolutely certain that the relatives of the evading person communicate with him in some way. Perhaps mail is received from him at an unknown drop. In any event, the investigator feels sure mail is being sent to the missing person.

How can the investigator get a peep at the addresses on outgoing envelopes after they are deposited in a letter box by the relatives?

If the matter is important enough to warrant shadowing, the wife or other relatives should be observed constantly to determine when mail is dropped in a box. When this is done, the investigator should *immediately* drop in the same box a couple of dozen ordinary blotters. The investigator should read the legend on the mail box to determine the time the carrier is due to remove its contents, and should return in time to anticipate the arrival of the carrier.

When the mail carrier arrives to empty the box, the investigator should identify himself and ask to see the last piece of mail *directly* under the layer made by the blotters. The mail dropped by the watched person can easily be picked out because the angles by which the letter falls will cause some part of it to be topmost under the blotters. The mails are in no way held up by this method, because after a quick but thorough perusal of the outside markings of the mail in question, it is handed back immediately to the carrier. If the investigator is confronted unexpectedly with the problem of isolating mail in a given box, torn pieces of newspapers, magazines, or anything else at hand, may be substituted effectively for the blotters.

The telephone company also presents a source of information easily available and one which often blazes the trail to the missing witness. In a situation similar to the one above described, if the wife or other relatives of the missing person have a telephone, the toll slips covering that particular number should be examined at the office of the telephone company. Frequently these slips present a record of frequent calls to a particular number in another location over a sustained period of time. This is a circumstance warranting immediate investigation of the number so frequently called.

An avenue for information not too often utilized but which has potential value for the investigator is that of interviewing a clergyman in a neighborhood where a missing person is known to have resided or where a member of his family is known to live during the time the investigator is operating. Quite often if the investigator tactfully explains that it will serve the ends of justice and that it will be to the best eventual interest of the missing man to disclose himself, the clergyman will lend his moral influence to prevail upon the subject to surrender if he is a fugitive, or to make his whereabouts known if he is a witness.

Once a witness is found and his story procured or the proper action taken, the investigator should maintain a suspense file and at intermittent intervals verify the whereabouts of the witness. This should always be done unless the case is closed immediately after the testimony of the witness and there can be no possible further need for him. If the investigator has procured a very important statement from a witness, it is wise to keep in touch with him.

Frequently an entire case is based on the testimony of one witness. The facts about which the witness will testify are known because his sworn statement has been procured. When the case comes to trial, however, it is often found that the witness has died or is seriously ill. If no continual liaison is kept with an important witness, he may move prior to trial and possibly will not be available when it is time to testify. If the investigator keeps the liaison with the witness active, however, and it is ascertained that the witness is seriously ill or anticipates leaving the jurisdiction, a preferential trial can be arranged if these facts are brought to the attention of the court. The trial then takes place while the witness is still available, being moved up toward the head of the court calendar because of the exigencies of the situation.

An informal, friendly liaison with the witness also will often serve the purpose of maintaining the good faith of the witness. Unfortunately it has developed many times that a witness upon whose testimony an all-trusting investigator based his company's entire case suffered a sudden suspicious lapse of memory shortly before the trial. This is a contingency of which an investigator must ever be cognizant.

It is the rare and unusual person indeed who does not have some form of documentary evidence concerning himself on file in some public agency. Actually, if laws and regulations were fully observed, every person in the United States would have some self-documentation on file at some time during his life. All states now require records of all births and deaths occurring within their borders. It may be found, however, that in some cases these provisions became effective in recent years, thus making it difficult in these instances to find documentation of events occurring prior to the time mandatory registration became effective.

A person who is born, lives, and dies without any record of his existence on earth must have been indigenous to the most primitive of backwoods hinterlands. There are too few such places in these United States today to make them a factor worth considering by the investigator.

Records of a person are kept about his birth, his entrance in school, arrests, marriage, fatherhood, divorce; his litigations, purchase and sale of real estate, inheritance or bequeathing of property; his buying or selling of a car, obtaining a driver's

license, registering for or entering military service; his voting
and running for office, leaving or entering the country.

When a person obtains a job the Social Security Board
ordinarily will have a record of this occurrence. If employed by
the government, complete employment records are available.
When a person is hospitalized, or when he has an accident at
his work, or any other accident in which an insurance company is involved, there will be records. Records are kept when
a person files an income-tax return either with the government
or the state; when he applies for permits of any sort; when he
is the recipient of rationing documents; when he takes a Civil
Service Examination; when he applies for a passport or naturalization; when he opens a charge account; when he signs a
lease; when he buys on the installment plan; when he borrows
money from a bank; when he applies for an insurance policy.
His name is recorded when he takes a trip on a common carrier having passenger lists; when he opens a bank account;
when he buys traveler's checks; when he has telephone service;
when he arranges for public utility service for his home, including electricity, gas, water or heat; when he registers in a hotel;
when he retires on a pension; when he is the recipient of relief
or other governmental or municipal benefits; when he rents a
safety deposit box in a bank; when he rents a post-office box.

Comprehensive records are kept when securities are bought
or sold. The cohesive organizations of labor make it mandatory
for practically every artisan or workingman to belong to a
union, and these organizations have routine records of their
members. All professional men must be licensed. Complete
records are on file covering all doctors, registered nurses, den-
tists, undertakers, lawyers, osteopaths, optometrists, certified
public accountants, chiropractors, architects, and veterinarians.
Many states require that persons in service trades that can be
classed as semiprofessional—such as plumbers, barbers, elec-
tricians, and beauty culturists—must be licensed.

Certain types of skills are recognized, and the men possessing them are licensed. In this field are found the licensed mariners with certificates attesting to their qualifications in seafaring, the schoolteacher, the realty broker, the private investigator, the auctioneer, the surveyor, and the engineer.

Most states provide for the licensing of food handlers or restaurant workers. All states provide for the licensing of liquor dispensers excepting those localities where the sale of intoxicating liquor is banned. Taxis and other vehicles carrying passengers, together with their operators, are especially licensed. Special licensing provisions exist in most states for gasoline filling stations, dance halls, cabarets, saloons, theaters, factories, stores, hotels, inns, and a host of other enterprises.

Most municipalities have ordinances governing the licensing of porters, salesmen, peddlers, guides, bellboys, and bartenders. Permits are issued for possession of firearms, for hunting, fishing, owning a dog.

Much more could be written to cite the potential records that may be kept about a person as he makes his way through life and that remain after the journey is culminated by the final record of all—the death certificate.

Some of the sources available for documentary investigation have been enumerated in detail because these fountainheads of information are veritable gold mines for the investigator, not only because of the data available but because documentary proof is the easiest to obtain and is often the most forceful. It should be noted that most of the written records pertaining to a person are in official archives rather than in private possession. Public offices are usually the most satisfactory source to consult, as most official records have a degree of permanency, and information requested in letter form by the investigator usually brings prompt response, because public offices are ably equipped to supply the desired information.

Since a man's life history from the cradle to the grave is

filed in official archives, a good investigator should know every file in these archives and where to find every phase of a man's recorded life. To attain this, he should familiarize himself with all the state and municipal bureaus and agencies in the territory in which he operates. The investigator should learn the functions of each department in his local government, and he should know by whom the numerous records are kept and where they can be inspected. Vital statistics, court data, licenses and permits, and other records are kept in different repositories in the different states. Sometimes a record that is available in the county seat in one state is available only in the state capital of another state.

Of all the public records to which reference has been made, one will be singled out for detailed explanation and emphasis because it is regarded as the greatest single source of enlightenment on the personal history and background of a subject.

This document is the *application* for marriage licenses (definitely to be distinguished from the marriage license and certificate). Many uninformed investigators unfortunately overlook this vital document in their investigations.

The uses of this document are multiple, and no other single record contains so much information or can be of so much aid, regardless of the purpose of the investigation. In applying for a marriage license, the prospective bride and groom must ordinarily fill out certain required data before the license is issued. There are minor differences in the information desired by the respective states, but in the main the requirements are similar.

In addition to the health report which most states require and which always gives the name of the applicant's doctor (that is, the one who gave the blood test and who may be the family physician) the following additional information appears for both applicants: (1) sample of handwriting as it appears on the signed application; (2) birthplace; (3) date of birth; (4) race; (5) occupation; (6) prior marital status; (7) names of parents and their nativity together with a statement as to whether they are alive or dead; (8) the address of parents; (9) the address of the applicant; (10) if prior marital status was indicated as "married," a statement as to how the prior marriage was dissolved.

The investigator can easily understand how valuable such leads are in an investigation. The additional documents in the same file, growing out of the marriage, will show the place where the marriage took place, the name of the clergyman or official performing the ceremony, and the names and addresses of the witnesses.

One of the elements of significant value in clues presented by the marriage file is that the file consists of statements made at a time and place where a person would not ordinarily lie unless contemplating bigamy. A person very rarely lies about his mother's name, for instance; hundreds of cases are known where although a fugitive married under an alias he gave his mother's correct name. A person may lie about his age in number of years, but oddly enough, he usually uses his actual birthday on records. It is obvious that the task of finding a person is made easier when the investigator is informed where his parents live, his occupation, his age, his doctor, his place of origin, his friends (who are generally the witnesses to the ceremony), and his clergyman. In addition to all these, a photostat will show a bona fide sample of his handwriting.

The avenues open to the investigator in locating a missing person are not limited to those set forth in this chapter. The alert, inquisitive investigator will discover new ways and means to unlock the door to the particular mystery he is seeking to solve. The fugitive or evading witness must be gifted with supernatural powers, however, if he can run the whole gauntlet of documentary pitfalls and vanish without leaving a trace.

CHAPTER FOUR

THE INTERVIEW

THE method of conducting an interview will depend to a very great extent on its purpose and the relationship of the person interviewed to the subject matter. The approach of the investigator to a woman whose husband has just been killed in an accident will be entirely different from the approach to a junk dealer who has been suspected of buying stolen machinery. The attitude and demeanor of the investigator should vary according to the case. It is impracticable to relate every conceivable type of investigation and the proper approach thereto. The investigator's God-given common sense should govern in each case. As the investigator gains in experience, he will develop an intuitive sense about which approach to take and will come to depend on it.

When the investigator first meets his subject, he should not arm himself immediately with notebook and pencil and start taking down information given by the subject. The investigator should first introduce himself by producing his credentials, at the same time explaining the reason for the visit. Unless the data submitted by the witness are involved and technical, the investigator should not write down notes as the interview progresses, but instead he should wait until the witness has finished his story. Then the investigator should state that he wishes to set down all the witness has related in the form of a statement. The investigator will then prepare the statement properly, and after it is completed, ask the witness to sign it.

It is easy to understand that if a notebook is flourished before the prospective witness immediately after he is encountered, before he knows what is going on and before his confidence is won, he is liable to become frightened, and he may find refuge in the old axiom "if you don't say anything, you don't say anything wrong."

It has been emphasized that the investigator should always have with him ample writing material. It is also suggested that the new investigator have in his possession sample statements taken in other cases to be used as guides when taking a statement himself. As a matter of fact, it is wise for any investigator to have such a sample statement in his possession at all times as a check against omitting important points when taking a statement under particularly trying conditions.

It is not possible to reduce to formula the common denominators of the rules of interviewing. Human beings are individuals, and their traits are too variable to be molded to exact pattern. The same general principles that motivate the other actions of human beings, however, are present in interviewing. Many psychological traits are present in practically all human beings when they are confronted with specific situations.

The investigator acting as interviewer should train himself to judge quickly the other person and his traits, at the same time being alert to his own traits, whims, and prejudices. It was pointed out earlier that the investigator should avoid being offensive in any way to a witness. The investigator should also regard himself as a party to the interview, which is really a conversation between two persons, and in thinking of himself in that way, the investigator should regard objectively everything about the witness. Unless this course is followed, it might be easy for the investigator to develop a prejudice against the witness which would color his questions, and as a result the investigator might find himself placing an interpretation on facts at variance with the truth.

The investigator who has previously "typed" his witness should have less difficulty in obtaining the desired information. Even the most co-operative type of witness, however, should be the subject of quick analysis by the investigator at the time of meeting. A witness may regard the investigator as a necessary evil. The investigator should overcome that barrier to obtaining full testimony by endeavoring to point out the witness's civic duty. For instance, the subject of divorce may be a delicate one with a witness whose faith does not recognize it, and the investigator should try to be cognizant of such a factor and tread easily where the circumstances require. Similarly an otherwise co-operative witness may destroy the value of his testimony because of racial prejudice. Persons having an antipathy for the use of liquor may give warped testimony if it relates to a person who drinks. In no instance involving a co-operative or disinterested witness should the investigator turn the interview into an inquisition, or make the witness feel as if the whole proceeding were an imposition.

The investigator is a fact-finder, and in no case should he impose his moral judgment upon the witness no matter what his own opinion. Many instances show that because of definite and rigorous feelings and prejudices a witness may lie about one phase of a case yet predominantly relate the truth. There is a distinction between the lie in an interview and the lie told in a courtroom on the witness stand. In court, the judge may direct that if a witness is found to be lying all his testimony may be disregarded. If one lie is discovered in a statement procured by an investigator, however, he may still use the other facts that are true to further his cause.

While an investigator should work with those tools that he has, it is often helpful to borrow a tool. It sometimes happens that an investigator knows beforehand that a particular witness may speak a language or be of a faith or disposition that will preclude the investigator from obtaining a satisfactory interview. In such a case it would not be amiss for the investigator to have an appropriate colleague interview the witness for him.

Whenever it is feasible it is wise for the investigator to operate in localities where he knows the psychology and customs of the inhabitants and where he himself has established a wide acquaintance resulting in a large number of potential informants.

During World War II an army officer from the Ozarks was investigating a case which necessitated interviewing an elderly Italian restaurateur located on the Brooklyn water front. The English of the investigator was flawless, his manner courteous, and his diction definitely the softest of Southern drawls. The Brooklyn proprietor seemed to be willing to co-operate, but his language was unknown to the investigator. After a few unsuccessful attempts to make himself understood, the army officer wrote a note which he gave to the witness, asking that a member of the family who could speak English bring the witness down to the army office the following morning for interrogation.

The witness took the note, glanced at it, and then excitedly pushed the investigator into a seat. The Italian then wrote a reply in perfect English asking what information the army officer wanted. The officer then wrote out each question, which was answered immediately in writing by the witness. At the conclusion of the "interview" the two beamingly shook hands, and the investigator departed with the desired information, each of his written queries having its own written answer. While this ending was fortunate, it could just as easily have resulted in a muddled impasse with the resultant loss of valuable time and possibly information to the army.

No investigator should ever promise a witness any reward or compensation for his testimony, *contingent upon the outcome of litigation*. If the witness ever refers to such an agreement with the investigator when he is testifying, it is "goodbye" for the investigator's case. It is very dangerous to the case of the investigator at any time if disclosure is made in court that a witness was paid for his testimony or for his time in court. Statutory subpoena fees for witnesses are presumed to cover any payment to the witness.

The cases of expert witnesses are exceptions. An expert or specialist is paid for testifying, but technically he is paid for the time he spends in analyzing and studying the subject matter to be introduced in the evidence about which he would later testify.

The investigator should never overlook the possible testimony of children. Most investigators are prone to pass by children as sources of information. Children are one of the best types of witnesses, popular impression to the contrary notwithstanding. A jury is more apt to believe an intelligent child than an adult. The investigator, however, should always qualify the child witness in the statement. He should not swear the child, but he should have the child briefly state at the beginning of the statement that he understands the difference between right and wrong, between lying and telling the truth, and that lying is doing wrong. If the child believes he will not go to heaven, if he believes he will go to hell, if he believes he will be struck by lightning when he tells a falsehood, the investigator should set forth exactly what the child's belief is. With this qualification the child will be allowed to testify. The general rules seems to be that the testimony of a child will be admitted if he knows the difference between right and wrong and is conscious of punishment for wrongdoing.

People are often sensitive about their personal lives. Questions as to their prior or current marital life, criminal backgrounds, poverty, or contagious diseases may seem to them unwarranted intrusions. The confidence of the witness should be gained, and he should be convinced that the investigator is not motivated by wanton curiosity but should be regarded as a doctor, a clergyman, or a lawyer when personal information is related.

In some cases a witness will be questioned in a place of business or in a home where others are present and frequently in an agony of embarrassment will not relate those private and personal incidents that may be necessary to the investigator's report. The investigator should always make every effort to interview the witness alone. If the home offers no private room, the investigator's car outside the door will supply needed privacy. If a car is not available, a walk to a neighborhood post office or library may help.

Another important reason why the investigator should seek to interview his witness in private is to offset the possibility of another person present at the interview later stating that the person interviewed did not understand the question or that there was some agreement not reflected in the written statement.

If it is not possible to interview the witness alone, it is always wise to place an additional paragraph at the bottom of the statement to the effect that one or more persons, as the case might be, were present during the taking of the statement and that all of the contents were understood by the witness and stated by him to be true. This additional statement is then signed by any others present, and they become corroborating witnesses. Sometimes the third person is asked to be a witness to the signature of the person interviewed, and the additional corroborating statement is submitted to him.

The investigator should always look thoroughly about the room where the interview is to take place for any untoward signs. The writer well remembers one incident when he interviewed the mother of a fugitive in a slovenly, one-room waterfront hovel. The interview was highly confidential. The mother, who was no more than forty and who reeked of gin, was interviewed at a kitchen table. The only other furniture in the room was a stove, a couple of chairs, and an unmade bed.

As the interview neared its close, the writer thought he detected a stir in the bunched-up, dirty bedding. He looked again, and there was definitely some movement. The mother was asked if anyone was in the bed. She said her little niece was there. The writer casually asked how old the little niece was, and he was told "twenty-two." This threw the entire investigation out of focus, and plans had to be made all over again because of the presence of the third party hidden in the bedding.

The necessity for alertness during the course of an interview cannot be overemphasized. The investigator should have his ears, eyes, and mind trained to take in every detail that might be important to him. A case in point may well illustrate the result of alertness on the part of one investigator. A man who was allegedly hurt by an automobile was suspected of being a "repeater" or chronic "flopper." He was interviewed by the insurance company representative. The keen-eyed investigator noticed that the initials in the claimant's hat band were at variance with the initials of his name. The investigator said nothing about this during the interview, but by successfully following the leads presented by this clue, the claimant was shown to have several aliases, with an accident under each alias. Last reports were that criminal proceedings were pending against him.

Nothing is "obvious" and nothing should ever be taken for granted by the investigator. One lawyer trying a crossing-accident case for a railroad company based most of his case on what he believed would be the crossing watchman's testimony. The watchman told the railroad's lawyer that he had waved his lantern frantically at the approaching automobile the night of the accident, but that the oncoming vehicle disregarded his warning and ploughed on past him into the side of a freight train traversing the crossing. On the witness stand, the frightened watchman admitted under cross-examination that he was in the course of refuelling his lantern when the warning gong sounded the approach of the train. When he saw the headlights of the oncoming automobile, he rushed out with the unlighted lantern and the stop sign in an effort to flag the car, which crashed into the side of the freight train.

The important point in this story is the fact that when the watchman was interrogated by the railroad company adjuster, since he was not asked if the lantern was lit, he did not volunteer the information that it was out. Had the railroad company known the facts it might have prepared the case in another fashion, or it might have settled with the plaintiffs instead of being caught in such an unenviable position during the trial.

From the standpoint of the investigator it doesn't matter if he is presenting a report in an affirmative case or in a defensive action. His chain of evidence should be as complete as possible with all the links connected. The investigator should always remember that a chain is as strong as its weakest link, but if one link goes, the chain breaks.

A common fallacy of investigators is to prepare a statement for the signature of a witness which is in the language of the investigator. This is erroneous and dangerous. A semiliterate witness who can barely sign his name will subject the investigator's cause to caustic examination and criticism when a high-sounding, English masterpiece bearing his signature is presented on his behalf. No statement procured from a witness is ever obtained for the purpose of being entered in a prose contest, nor is it supposed to be a masterpiece of English literature. The statement should be as closely as possible in the language of the witness, even to the use of slang, or "dese," "dem" and "dose." As long as the statement is comprehensible, it will serve its purpose as a conveyor of the facts. If it is necessary to use vulgarity to express the thoughts of the witness, this means should be employed because its ultimate purpose is for a court of law where vulgar expression is admissable in the interests of justice.

An investigator should keep in mind the specific scope of the investigation he is charged with making, but on the other hand he should realize that because of individual circumstances certain questions take on added moment, and he should be cognizant and tolerant of emphasis placed on seemingly unimportant or irrelevant matters by the witness. Thus the height of a building takes on added significance to a sufferer of heart trouble, a question as to birthplace means much to a naturalized citizen, and a question of college degrees means much to a person who has been expelled from college.

An average interview should be a smooth interchange of thought. If the testimony is to relate to an accident or an event, the good investigator will have available printed outlines or photographs of streets or buildings which the witness will initial, and then reference will be made to the descriptive parts of the sketches or photographs in the statement. In important cases, papier-mâché models have been made of buildings and rooms, the witness placing his initials on each object referred to in the statement.

Events ordinarily meriting the attention of an investigator are high lights in the life of the witness, who will talk excitedly and continually to all and sundry who will listen to what he has to say about an event he has just observed. That is why time is of such importance in visiting witnesses in certain types of case.

These witnesses are willing to talk; in fact they want to talk and they welcome the investigator. As time goes on, however, the interest of the witness wavers and dies out, and his memory dims as his enthusiasm wanes. This type of witness, after being reached, should be allowed to "bubble" all he wants to without interruption. After he finishes his story, the investigator may then ask the pertinent questions still not covered.

While the co-operative witness is not reluctant to submit his evidence, the impersonal and impartial witness may sometimes present a callous indifference to the extent that the evidence he gives is sparse and sketchy. This type of witness volunteers nothing, and while he may answer those questions put to him, pulling teeth would seem like an easier job than extracting information from him. The investigator should seek to win over this type of witness by establishing some form of common bond as previously described. Sometimes an appeal to the civic duty and obligations of the witness as a citizen and resident of the community may inspire him to talk. No witness, regardless of his nature, should ever be threatened or intimidated.

The most difficult information to obtain is that elicited from the reluctant, non-co-operative witness. While he may not be threatened, enticed, or entrapped, an impartial explanation of the situation in which he is involved, with a mention of the resulting penalty to any person convicted of a similar wrongdoing, may sometimes bring forth the desired information.

In criminal, as well as all other investigations, no investigator should ever promise immunity of any sort. He has no legal right to do so, and only the court may affix sentence. It is a matter of common knowledge, however, that a joint defendant in a conspiracy case will often be prevailed upon to turn state's evidence and become a witness for the prosecution against the other violator. In return, he generally receives a lesser sentence for his crime.

In a technical sense, no judge or court can be a party to such a proceeding. The judge may or may not follow the recommendation of the prosecuting attorney. In a practical sense, however, the court almost always does so when a defendant has been co-operative. The investigator, however, who interviews a defendant in a case in which prosecution may be entailed should never promise to effect or consummate the "deal." The inducement to the witness in such cases is the statement by the investigator that he will advise the proper prosecuting authorities that the witness has been co-operative, and that this fact should be taken into consideration.

The motivations present in various types of interviews are so manifold that at best only brief generalizations can be made. Sometimes an investigator contacting a non-co-operative witness will relate an incident and ask whether it is true or not. This is not good interviewing because the investigator is disclosing a possible confidential matter by his statement of facts to one who may misuse it. Rather, the witness should be asked to relate what he knows about the matter in question. Because of such careless questioning, many investigators are in turn used by their informants. There are many cases of unlawful activities on record showing that an investigator, seeking confirmation of some information, related the details of suspected continuing violation to a supposedly trustworthy informant who in turn warned the suspected violators that their activities were known.

One of the common methods of extracting information is by the so-called "friend-and-enemy system." This system is used in both civil and criminal investigations and applies equally to reluctant and disinterested witnesses. When this method is being used, two investigators will interview a witness. One will be gross, tough, demanding, insulting, uncouth, and caustic. In general his attitude will be such as to cause the witness discomfort, with a resulting desire to throw him out. The other investigator will be the direct antithesis of his tough partner. His attitude will be that of a long-suffering lesser half of the partnership, and he will apparently be on the receiving end of the tough one's bombast, together with the witness.

After some time of getting nowhere, the tough investigator remembers he has an appointment and leaves the interview to his mild partner with the parting admonition that time has been wasted in trying to get information in a "nice" way, darkly hinting that there were "other" means of extracting the desired information from the witness. All this byplay, of course, is in the presence of the witness.

After the tough investigator leaves, the meek, kind partner turns to the witness with some such remark as "If you don't like him, what do you think of me? I have to work with him all day!" The remaining investigator will be sympathetic, understanding, and kind, and will convey the impression that he is an ally of the witness against the departed investigator. Very frequently when this approach is used, the remaining investigator will obtain the entire story from the witness because a common level has been established—that of mutual dislike of a third person. The interview generally ends with the witness commiserating with the investigator for being compelled to work with a person as obnoxious as his partner.

The question of the choice of partners, incidentally, is of paramount importance to the investigator. Many investigations are conducted by teams of two investigators. When criminal action is contemplated, this is always advisable because of the element of mutual protection and corroboration.

Involved investigations will frequently necessitate two investigators working together for months, day after day. There are times, when they travel away from their homes, when they are compelled not only to work together, but to eat their meals together and to share the same room. It can readily be understood that if the relationship between the two men is not a congenial one, such close association can become trying and nerve-racking. It is a sad commentary that thousands of teams work together every year without speaking a word to each other that does not involve their duties.

If at all feasible, when there is to be joint investigation, teams of investigators with propensities for getting along together should be selected. The investigator should keep his eyes wide open before such a choice is made, but once the selection is completed, and the joint enterprise is begun, each partner should keep his eyes half closed where the other one is concerned.

The written statement is the basis of perpetuating in unchanged form the evidence adduced by a witness. There is, however, a certain kind of witness from whom a written statement is not necessary, for instance, a person who is in an official or semi-official capacity and whose organizations are in possession of records germane to the issues in the case. Thus, postmasters, bankers, police officials, government officials, utility-company officials, and others who are in custody of their organization's records need be interviewed verbally only, and excerpts may be made from the records. The information contained in the documents is at the place of repository permanently, regardless of whether the official remains its custodian or not. If the official knows certain pertinent facts not connected with his position, however, or not reflected in the records, a statement from him should then be obtained.

The investigator should always obtain the exact title of the official's position so that when it is necessary to subpoena the desired records, the subpoena may be returnable to the proper custodian by title rather than by name. The reason for this is, of course, that in the event the official who was the custodian at the time of the interview is no longer in the employ of the organization, the information will be available at the time of the trial.

It cannot be emphasized too strongly that the investigator

must always cultivate his business acquaintances so that he receives the best possible co-operation from officials. It should never be necessary for a good investigator to go to a public bureau in his territory to inspect documents. He should know someone in that office well enough to get a résumé of the contents of the documents over the telephone.

When an investigator is about to interview a witness who is an unknown quantity and whose testimony may be very material, it is often wise to learn something about the person to be interviewed before the contact is actually made. The potential witness should be unaware of this, of course. The investigator should be circumspect in making inquiry about a potential witness so that there is no possibility of a reflection being cast on his character. This is doubly true in the case of a woman.

In conducting the preliminary investigation the investigator should not relate the facts of the case nor state why or how the witness is involved. He should merely ascertain those facts about the subject that he seeks to know. There is no need to disclose the entire purpose of the investigation in order to obtain the secondary information.

The mail carrier is generally a key person to interview concerning persons in his territory and can usually be relied upon to keep a confidence. Both the newsboy and the rent collector often can supply helpful information. The corner grocery store, the local barber shop, and the neighborhood beauty parlor are surprising sources of information, but the investigator must be wary and wise in tapping any of these sources because of the human tendency to gossip. He defeats his own purpose, and sometimes dangerously, if he does not conduct this somewhat casual sleuthing in a dignified manner that precludes the possibility of gossip. Policemen are fine informants for this sort of help. In rural areas the state police are excellent and reliable contacts. The police officers usually

know their territory thoroughly, offer fine co-operation, and in
rural areas will frequently supply transportation to an investigator. A milkman or a meter reader for a utility company are
possible sources of information. The clergyman for the local
church will generally know the subject well if he is a member
of his congregation. The amount of help from these and
similar sources is very great if the investigator is wise enough
to use it.

Sometimes it is wise for the investigator to fortify himself
with documentary information about a witness he is to interview. This may prove of value if he wants to determine the
veracity of the witness during an interview.

To illustrate, assume the investigator has asked the witness
the same question several times to learn if the witness has
fabricated the answers (because he might vary them with each
reply), but in every case the witness gives the same answer.
The investigator does not know the answer. He was not present when the event occurred, but the witness was, and it is
important to know if he is telling the truth. The investigator
will then deliberately ask the witness specific questions to
which he already knows the answer. If he has obtained data
from the witness's application for marriage license, he may ask
his birthday, birthplace, mother's name, father's name, date of
marriage, and other data appearing on the application.

The investigator will watch the witness closely as he asks
these questions, and he will form an opinion about how the
witness reacts when answering a question truthfully. After asking about ten questions and receiving the answers which he
knows to be true, the investigator should ask the eleventh
question, one to which he does not know the answer. If the
demeanor and attitude of the witness do not change when
answering this question, the investigator can feel almost certain that he is telling the truth. If, however, the witness answering the eleventh question lights a cigarette, blinks his eyes,

crosses or uncrosses his legs, or in any way acts in a manner at variance with his conduct when giving truthful answers, the investigator may reasonably infer the witness is not answering the eleventh question truthfully.

The foregoing suggestion of going to the witness fortified with information about him can be of invaluable assistance for other purposes. If an investigator obtains a complete dossier about a dubious witness preparatory to contact, the available information can be of inestimable aid in breaking down the resistance of the subject.

It may seem like a waste of time for the investigator to obtain information that in itself serves no purpose. That is not the case, however. Assume that an investigator is seeking to obtain important information from a witness who is adamant in his refusal to talk. The investigator then can seemingly lose his patience and tell the witness many things he knows about him. The astounded witness usually will wonder how the investigator ever obtained the name of the minister who married him twenty years ago, or how the investigator knows the exact place and date of his birth, or how the investigator knows the name of his father, who may have been dead for thirty years. The investigator can pull a great many more family secrets out of his hat if he has made the necessary preliminary contacts in the neighborhood. He can then tell the witness that he can find the information he seeks elsewhere with the expenditure of some time, adding that he would of course have to report the witness as unco-operative and as refusing to disclose information. When this foundation is laid, the witness will frequently break down and say that as long as the investigator knows about everything, he may as well tell the rest. He then usually relates the story sought by the investigator.

Quite frequently an investigator will be asked by a witness

what will happen after the evidence is submitted. The investigator can easily slip out of that question, if he does not choose to amplify, by stating that he is merely a fact-finding agent, and that he does not make any determination, as that rests with a higher authority.

The investigator should never allow himself to look bored or indifferent during an interview. The investigation may be a casual one to him, but very often it is of paramount importance to the person being interviewed, who is generally aware of the deep human emotions that may lie behind the investigation in which he may be playing a vital part.

During the course of an interview an investigator should fix the events of the interview in his mind. He may be called upon to testify about particular occurrences months or years after they happened. In an effort to discredit the memory of an investigator, opposing counsel may ask him what he ate for breakfast on a particular day, perhaps a year before, or what he wore, or the color of his hat. The investigator should of course state that he does not remember. It would be foolhardy to burden one's memory by recollection of such unimportant things. The triumphant attorney will then ask, perhaps sarcastically, "And why do you remember the events at that interview so well—that is also a year ago." The reply for the investigator, of course, is that he fixed those events occurring at the interview in his mind because they were important and because he expected to be questioned about them.

The investigator should also avoid relative conclusions based on erroneous observations by the witness. A witness five feet tall, for instance, might refer to another person five feet six inches in height as tall, or a person six feet four inches tall might refer to a man of five feet ten inches as short. If a witness describes a man of one hundred and fifty pounds who was in company with two other men each weighing about one hundred and ten pounds, he will probably call him very fat. The investigator must be alert to such observations and realize they have no factual value.

The investigator should also have a general knowledge of mental abnormalities so as to differentiate between an insane person and a psychopathic witness. The latter may have certain abnormalities yet possess a very keen intelligence. It is always advisable that two investigators be present when an abnormal person is interviewed, especially when hysteria is present.

The investigator should train himself to be a good listener even though his patience at times becomes sorely tried. This is especially important if the witness has a grudge or complaint, real or fancied. If the witness is genuinely disturbed or grief-stricken, the therapy of "talking oneself out" not only helps the witness but places the investigator in the light of a friend if he listens sympathetically. A subject who is troubled when talking about deeply personal problems may sometimes fall into an embarrassing silence. The investigator should respect that silence and not break it without good reason. Usually the witness will resume talking after he has marshalled his emotions and thoughts. The investigator should be careful to distinguish irrelevant rambling from heartfelt emotion before making any attempt to curb the talkative witness.

Previous emphasis has been placed on the value of privacy when conducting an interview. Physical setting in general is important, and distracting noises such as telephone bells, interruptions by other persons, or mail deliveries should be kept at a minimum during the course of an interview. The witness should have the undivided attention of the investigator if the latter is to attain the undivided confidence of the witness.

The five W's should always be in the mind of an investigator during the course of an interview. They are: "WHO did WHAT, WHEN, WHERE, and WHY?"

CHAPTER FIVE

THE STATEMENT AND THE REPORT OF INVESTIGATION

A "STATEMENT" is the reduction to writing of the mutual thoughts of the witness and the investigator. In certain situations it is more desirable to procure a sworn statement. If so, the investigator should have the power to administer oaths, and he should always have the venue present on the upper left-hand corner of the first page of the statement. Sometimes it may be more effective to have the oath actually administered by a third person even if the investigator has the power to do so. This may serve to enhance the importance of the facts in the statement in the minds of a jury, and it may serve to discount the possible inference that the investigator who took the statement did not actually administer the oath.

In some cases, notably where the subject is a defendant, or where there is a suspicion that he may become a defendant in criminal proceedings, it may become advisable to administer the constitutional admonition. This need not be in any involved legal terminology but may be in the informal phraseology of the witness himself. The constitutional admonition should state that the signer realizes the constitution gives him the right to refuse to answer any questions; that he makes the statement freely and voluntarily, without any threats or promises of reward or immunity; and that he also realizes that anything he says may be used against him. Such a statement is sufficient to meet the legal requirements.

While it is customary to place the oath or constitutional admonition at the beginning of the written statement, placing it at the end of the document will not invalidate it. Frequently a witness will be frightened into a refusal to sign any statement if the admonition and warning are related to him first. Actually, the investigator must obtain a statement and signature at the proper psychological moment in the interview. If the investigator concludes the interview and still does not feel the time is ripe to start recording the conversation because of the attitude of the witness, he should not attempt it. Instead, he should engage the witness in general conversation if possible until the hysteria, resentment, or other obstacle is overcome. It is repeated that the investigator should first orally interrogate the witness and procure the entire story before starting to prepare the formal statement.

While the constitutional admonition is most generally used in recording the confessions and admissions of persons who may later be accused of a crime, many investigators use it occasionally in purely civil statements. It is sometimes felt that the impact of such a statement will impress the witness with the seriousness of his statement, and that it will act as a powerful motivator in procuring the truth.

In the conversation preliminary to writing out the actual statement, the investigator should be thoroughly informed of all the facts, including dates, names, and places. Frequently there may be so many dates and places mentioned that the investigator could not possibly remember them all when the time arrived to begin preparation of a statement. As these data are given, therefore, the investigator should make a note of them on a piece of paper or in an inconspicuous notebook, the smaller the better. Figures referring to sums of money and mathematical calculations are difficult to remember and should be so noted also. The notebook or paper will then serve as a reference when it is time to incorporate the facts into the statement. If this procedure is followed, it will obviate the necessity of changing or adding to the statement because of revelations the witness has forgotten to repeat.

After the preliminary interview is completed and the oral information is to be reduced to writing, the investigator should state in an offhand and casual manner that he wishes to record the events related while they are still fresh in his mind.

The signed statement is the crux of most completed investigations, and its correctness in form and content is of paramount importance. If the investigator prepares an unsworn statement, the document should commence with the identifying data, the name, address, and age of the witness and any relationship or connection of the witness to the subject of the investigation.

After this is set forth, comes the body of the statement. This should include the entire statement of facts as related by the witness, written in his own language. It is important to remember all statements should be written in the first person, just as if the witness were actually seated on a witness stand stating "I saw this" or "I did that."

The body of the statement should be in narrative form in chronological sequence. Regardless of how the information unfolded during the interview, the statement should begin with the oldest point of pertinent information and work up gradually to the latest event. The witness, of course, may not have related his story in this order, but the investigator should break it down in orderly sequence in his own mind before reducing the information to writing. While the investigator should employ the language of the witness as much as possible in preparing the statement, paraphrasing is permissible if it is not too radical a departure.

Upon completion of the body of the statement containing the pertinent information, the investigator writes the closing paragraph. This is generally a statement by the witness that he has read the foregoing statement; that he has signed each page thereof; that the number of pages he read and signed was (to be specified); that he has made the necessary corrections; and that the contents of the statement are true. This is followed by his signature and the date.

The greatest problem confronting the investigator is whether or not the statements procured will "hold up" in the trial. All too frequently witnesses do not choose to back up their written statements, and the reason most frequently advanced by these backsliders on the witness stand is that they did not understand thoroughly the meaning of the statements signed by them.

It is therefore the responsibility of the investigator to forestall such a contingency by foreseeing all possible exigencies and appropriately coping with them.

While a signature on each page of a statement is a safeguard —which incidentally protects the witness because signing the last page of a multipage statement would not bar an unscrupulous investigator from inserting a page which the witness never saw—there are other means of protecting the statement.

For instance, many investigators will often deliberately make minor errors in writing out a statement—at least one error on each page—so that the witness will cross out the error and insert the correct data in his own handwriting. The witness could hardly claim thereafter he did not read the statement nor understand its text.

A statement by the witness in his own handwriting, "I have read this statement," prior to signing it also helps.

The investigator should be careful to find out if the witness can actually read and write or if he merely understands verbal English. If the latter is the case, the text of the closing paragraph should then be changed to "I have had read to me, etc." The reason why the witness cannot or does not read the statement should be given. If the witness is blind, it is wise for a friend or member of the family to read the statement to him, and the person who does this should make an appropriate statement to that effect. Any disability of the witness that might reflect on his possible understanding of the contents of the statement should be explained as should also how the difficulty was overcome.

If the statement was given to the investigator through an interpreter, the closing paragraph should state that the document was read by the interpreter. The end of the statement is elastic and should be made to fit the varying situations. The interpreter should make an additional statement underneath the signature of the witness that he fully understands English and the language interpreted, and that he has completely and fairly interpreted the document.

Frequently after a witness has related his story and it is reduced to writing he suffers a change of heart and becomes timid or recalcitrant, refusing to sign the statement. If possible, the investigator should have a colleague present at that time. The statement should be read back to the witness, and if the witness affirms that the contents are true but that he will not sign it, the two investigators should sign a statement underneath the unsigned story to this effect:

> This statement was read to John Doe at his home, 135 King Street, Charleston, S. C., on this first day of October, 1946, by Investigator Patrick Smith. John Doe stated, in our presence, the contents of the statement as read to him were true but he refused to affix his signature thereto.
>
> *Signed*—Patrick Smith, Investigator
> *Signed*—William Jones, Investigator

An investigator should *never* sign his name as a witness to a statement he procures, with the exception of the example shown above.

A clever stratagem to obtain a signature from a reluctant witness is as follows: If a witness refuses to sign a statement with the explanation that he does not wish to embroil himself with the law or that he does not wish to take sides in a dispute, he may be asked to sign a statement to *that* effect. Frequently he consents to do so. In a case of that kind, a statement like the following should be used:

> I have read the above statement and I know all the contents thereof to be true. Because I do not care to become involved in this affair, however, I refuse to sign the statement.
>
> Signed—John Doe
Acknowledgment

It is obvious that this type of acknowledgment is just as satisfactory as the conventional signature to the statement.

A court reporter or stenographer who transcribes notes may often be asked to sign a statement that the notes were correctly transcribed, and the stenographic notes should be carefully filed.

Typewritten copies of statements should be discouraged, and no copies of the statement procured by the investigator should be relinquished to the witness if this can be avoided. If an adversary is present in the investigation there is a possibility of the copy falling into his hands. He will then know the facts upon which the case is predicated, which might be a disadvantage to the investigator.

Often an investigator will call upon the services of a public stenographer in a hotel or other public place to prepare a particularly important statement. If copies are necessary, the investigator should be careful to ask for the carbon paper used by the stenographer. This may appear to be overcautious but if the case is important enough to exercise every precaution against leaks, the carbon paper may present a leak that will ruin the case. If new carbon paper is used to make copies of a document, the exact replica of the data appearing on the paper is clearly decipherable on the carbon. There are known instances of stenographers disclosing confidential data by this means. This method is especially useful to unscrupulous secretaries when involved calculations or technical formulas are copied—data that are not easily remembered.

Copies of important statements should be clearly marked and filed so as not to be disassociated from the correct file or from the investigator in charge of the case. Any receptacle for documents such as brief cases or attaché cases should bear the investigator's name and address so that it may be returned if it is lost.

The investigator will find many witnesses vacillating or uncertain during the interview. Sometimes the witness is honest in his uncertainty and sometimes deliberately evasive. Whatever the motive may be, the misgivings or uncertainty reflected in the mind of the investigator or the contradictions made and rectified by the witness should not appear in the body of the statement. They are to be preserved in the mind of the investigator for other action to be discussed. Factual data only are inserted in the statement. It should never reflect an issue between the investigator and the witness.

The investigator will find it is advisable to have the witness read the completed statement orally prior to signing. If in the reading the witness should hesitate and stumble in pronouncing a word, the investigator should realize a grave error has been committed by him including a word or phrase not understood or spoken by the witness. If this should happen on the witness stand, the statement may become not only worthless but extremely damaging.

Joint statements from two or more people who wish to testify to the same facts should not be taken. In a court, witnesses do not testify jointly. Each person appears on the witness stand individually, and if joint statements were taken, all sorts of technical difficulties could arise, such as the impeachment of one of the witnesses to a joint statement. No two persons who witness an occurrence will see it in exactly the same light, and the documents carry more weight if taken individually, alike on all basic facts, yet not identical.

While the investigator should endeavor to have the body of the statement clear, concise, and in conformity with the technical requirements of the rules of evidence, it is not always possible to do this. There are certain well-defined rules pertaining to the admissibility of evidence. These rules will be discussed later. Testimony that is extraneous to the issue, or is not relevant material, or is not admissible in evidence should not be included ordinarily in the statement.

The difficulty is that the witness does not know the rules of evidence. The investigator should gently guide the witness to relate only those facts or occurrences that are germane to the issue. When the witness insists upon rambling and relating a lot of hearsay, however, the investigator should accept the irrelevant data rather than antagonize him and risk losing all the information. When the investigator renders his report later he can omit the extraneous material.

Many witnesses who confess to a crime will seek to explain their misdeeds by justification which may be inadmissible as testimony, but rather than chance losing the confession, the investigator should accept the irrelevant data. The witness often thinks he has an excuse for his misdeeds, and were the investigator not listening to the alleged explanation, the witness might not confess the wrongdoing.

For example, a woman was charged with stealing twelve family-allowance checks issued on the military service of her brother. These checks were sent to the brother's wife who was working away from home. The sister took the monthly checks, forged the wife's name, and cashed them. When she was apprehended, the sister admitted the forgeries, but stated the wife was not entitled to the checks anyway because she was running around with other men. The first part of her statement is the confession—very relevant—while the latter part is immaterial. Yet the sister might not have confessed in this case unless she explained why she committed the crime. All her explaining, therefore, had to be inserted in the statement, although that part which was immaterial could not be used at the trial as it was not legally admissible.

A witness should always state the source of his information. Frequently an over-eager witness will represent a statement as factual which in reality had its inception in what his best friend told him. This type of statement is valueless.

The investigator should never incorporate in a statement a witness's comment that he has read some other person's statement, found it to be true, and desires to make it his own. The investigator should not be in the profession if he lacks the initiative to procure the supporting or corroborating statement from the other witness.

In citing an exhibit which the witness produces or to which he refers, great care should be taken that this exhibit is made an integral part of the statement. The witness should always sign and date the exhibit, and there should be a proper co-ordinating explanation in the statement explaining the particular exhibit. If the witness identifies more than one exhibit, each should be given an identification number so that when reference is made in the statement to the exhibits they will be referred to by identification number and there will be no question which exhibit is meant. The signature of the witness on the exhibit and his explanation and signature in the statement identify the exhibit as an integral part of the statement.

If a witness is asked to identify a photograph, several should be submitted to him, and he should pick the photograph in question out of the group, with proper explanation and reference made to it in the statement. If one person in a group photograph is to be identified, the witness should place his initials over that person's head.

Frequently one photograph which has already been identified by one witness will be shown to another for identification. If it is not deemed advisable to have the current witness know that the photograph has been identified previously, it is wise to have two photographs. If that is not feasible, the first witness should make the proper identification on the reverse side of the photograph. When it is shown to the current witness, the face on front of the picture is exhibited and the identification on the rear is not obvious. Sometimes a piece of paper may be lightly pasted over the prior identification if it is on the front of the photograph. When the current witness signs his name on the front of the photograph a dual identification is accomplished without either identifying person being cognizant of the other's action.

The question-and-answer form of statement is used by some investigators. While it is as legally acceptable as the narrative form of statement, it is not so widely used, chiefly because it does not allow the witness full rein of expression. In certain cases, as in the taking of depositions, or in pinning down an evasive witness to a specific reply, it may be more advantageous than the narrative statement.

No investigator is ever judged by what he does, but by what the reviewer or judge believes he has done. Accepting this as true, the investigator will understand the extreme importance of the "report of investigation."

Many an investigator has performed a praiseworthy job in investigating a case only to find that his efforts were almost in vain because he was unable to set forth in complete, concise, and comprehensive form the results of his investigation. The report of investigation is a document which emanates from the investigator as distinguished from the statement which emanates from the witness. This report is the vehicle whereby the result of the investigation is conveyed to the proper authority for further action or disposition.

Uniformity is necessary in report-writing. The field of investigation is so complex and varied, however, that several forms have developed for reporting similar types of investigation. Thus the numerous governmental activities, each dealing with a specific phase of law enforcement, have their respective forms for reports of·investigation. Within any one department, the reports are uniform. Similarly, various private concerns have their uniform types of report, shaped to fit their own requirements.

The investigator's report of investigation becomes a living, vital document when it bursts into life at the proper time. It may precipitate a trial; it may send a man to jail; it may stop a cheat from obtaining property; it may pay someone sufficient money to change a way of life; it may make a happy marriage; it may unmake an unhappy marriage. The contents of the investigator's report are of the utmost importance to those persons who are its subjects.

While the statement of the witness is written in the first person, the report of the investigator is always written in the third person. It should be written in chronological sequence from the inception of the original overt acts which created the points in issue—and these should be cited—through the actual elements of the investigation. It should be impersonal, unbiased, accurate, concise, complete, and truthful. Overstatement or understatement of fact should be avoided. The words used should convey the exact meaning they are intended to convey. While brevity is recommended, it should not be such as to sacrifice facts which should be included.

The opening paragraph should be introductory, stating briefly the preliminary events which led up to the creation of the issue necessitating investigation and naming the persons involved.

The report should be in narrative form unfolding the story from its beginning to the completion of the investigation. It is to be a story relating what the subjects and the witnesses did.

The investigator should learn to distinguish the facts from the clues. Clues may develop into admissible evidentiary facts. The facts are included in the report, but the clues are not. For instance, the investigator seeks to find John Doe at a given address. Upon arriving at the address, the investigator learns that John Doe moved to a neighboring city. This has nothing to do with the points in issue in the case. It is merely a clue. When the investigator goes to the city named, he may interview the postmaster for further information as to the whereabouts of the witness. This is also a clue, immaterial to the merits of the case. When the postmaster gives the investigator the exact address where he actually finds John Doe, however, the contact with Doe starts the chain of facts.

When the investigator prepares his report of investigation on the case he should state, "John Doe was interviewed at his home, 135 Boylston Street, Boston, Mass., on 15 Oct., 1946. His signed statement was procured, which is submitted herewith as exhibit 'Y.' In this statement Doe stated, '— —' etc." What the witness stated should be paraphrased and set forth only as to the admissible, relevant, and pertinent facts. These are the facts that are germane to the issue. There is no place in the report for the mere details such as how John Doe was found.

In procuring the statement from John Doe, the investigator may have been forced to record much extraneous, immaterial data injected by the witness, but the investigator should relate in his report only those facts which would be admissible in a court of law, and the irrelevant data should be omitted.

The investigator should avoid overstatements indicating a witness to be more culpable than appears from the facts. The investigator may sometimes in his enthusiasm color the report of investigation to such an extent that the significance of the facts as given by the witness is no longer recognizable. This is a foolhardy and dangerous practice.

Reports of investigation may be signed jointly by any number of investigators because a consolidated report may reflect the isolated activities of many persons acting independently of one another. Their efforts are later pieced together in one comprehensive report. This is distinguished from the practice of having witnesses submit statements individually and not jointly.

Although varying types of reports of investigation are prescribed by different organizations, most of them require the investigator's conclusions, which are inferences from proved facts. These conclusions are set forth, however, under a separate heading properly labeled, distinct from the cold, bare facts which must stand alone. There should never be a welding of the two. Facts must always stand by themselves on their own merits and must never be colored by conclusions set forth as facts.

Some reports of investigation may also require that the investigator set forth his recommendations for subsequent action.

A report of investigation should contain only the positive facts which clarify the points in issue. Negative elements are omitted. If the investigator contacted Mary Smith because he believed she was in possession of certain information that could be of aid to him, and if it developed she knew nothing about the issues, Mary Smith need not be mentioned in the report.

In the unfolding of an involved investigation there may be many leads which the investigator must check. If, upon being followed through, the leads turn into blind alleys and disclose no constructive information, they die as leads, and no reference should be made to them in the report of investigation.

Yet if an important point is not entirely cleared up by the

report of investigation, the reviewer might inquire why an obvious clue was not followed. There is nothing in the report to indicate that the investigator exhausted this lead with no results, because nothing positive was accomplished toward clarification of the issues. If, however, the investigator keeps a "contact" list covering all persons he interviewed even though no helpful information was obtained, and if he submits this list with the report, it will indicate that the investigator followed through on leads albeit with negative result. An appended list of names and dates of contact obviates the necessity of cluttering up the report of investigation with useless negative information and at the same time preserves the record of contacts for reference.

Another incidental or supplementary report which may be submitted with the report of investigation is the "confidential memorandum." This report sheds light on the human side of the investigation without detracting from the cold, legalistic, factual, report. It is recommended that the confidential memorandum be used as widely as possible.

Its uses are many. In addition to setting forth mitigating circumstances in criminal proceedings to present the prosecuting officials with a complete picture, it also serves to record any other impressions of the investigator. Impressions are not facts and cannot be part of the formal report of investigation. Yet, if the investigator feels a witness is evasive or lying, he should so state in his memorandum so that undue weight should not be attached to the testimony; preparations for trial may consequently take a different tack entirely. Many reviewing authorities are as much guided by the confidential memorandum as they are by the report of investigation, even though the memorandum is not factual.

Information that may be included in it is wide and varied, of course. For instance, a witness when interviewed might be ill, with the resultant danger he may not be available for trial.

A notation of this condition properly belongs in the confidential memorandum, as do the investigator's arguments about the issues should he choose to be argumentative.

Some witnesses or their attorneys might be so powerful politically in a community that the courts or jury would lean toward them. Certain litigants might be "tear jerkers" because of their appearance, or their possession of hordes of children and dependent relatives. This might command sympathy verdicts. Any information such as this, basically extraneous from the points in issue and definitely not admissible testimony, should nevertheless be noted and forwarded to the reviewing authorities in the memorandum.

An outline of the form of report of investigation commonly used by the Federal Bureau of Investigation follows using imaginary names and circumstances:

FEDERAL BUREAU OF INVESTIGATION

This case originated at　　　Miami, Fla., 1 July 1946
Miami, Fla.　　　　　　　　File No.—1776

Report made by—John E. Jones

Report made at	Date when made	Period Covered	Character of Case
Miami, Fla.	1 July 1946	1 June 1946 to 1 July 1946	Servicemens' Dependents Allowance Act.

TITLE
Mary Belting, alias Jane Driscoll,
alias Sylvia Rogers, alias Toby Cline.

SYNOPSIS
(Under this heading is included a short synopsis of facts indicating how the case arose and the various facts disclosed to the time the investigation is undertaken by the investigator.)

DETAILS

(Under this heading is included the report of investigation as developed by the investigator for the period covered by the report.)

Approved and forwarded

_____

Special Agent in Charge

CHAPTER SIX

SHADOWING, OBSERVATION, TAILING, AND ROPING

IN MANY instances, tailing and shadowing will develop the evidence by which the suspect is shown irrevocably to be involved in the perpetration of a crime, or in the commission of a questionable overt act.

There is no certainty in life about anything except death. Investigation is no exception. In order to minimize the risk of uncertainty in the solution of a problem the good investigator should play his percentages and use every card available to him so that he stacks the law of averages to such an extent that most of its decisions break in his favor. The four aces in the investigative deck are shadowing, observation, tailing, and roping. Even the toughest cases can be beaten by this hand.

Shadowing, as the name implies, obligates the investigator to become the shadow of the subject. As the shadow never leaves its caster, so must the investigator never leave his quarry. Shadowing is a type of observation involving persons. Observation in general may apply to persons, premises, vehicles, animals—in fact, to anything that can be detected by the senses.

A close tail is a form of shadowing put into effect to observe all the actions of a subject every minute of the day. The very minuteness of the observation creates the risk of being recognized or "made" by the subject. In this form of shadowing, two, three, or more investigators can be used effectively, depending upon the importance of the tail and the degree of effort that is to be exerted in not being "made."

A loose tail is a form of shadowing used when a general impression or picture is sought to be obtained of a subject's life or activities over a protracted period of time. In this form of tail the investigator may perform his duties at intermittent intervals.

Roping is also a form of observation by which the investigator goes undercover. He drops his identity as an investigator and assumes a new personality. While in the assumed status, the investigator wins the confidence of the suspect and endeavors to obtain the information which would ordinarily have been difficult for him to procure openly as an investigator. It is a form of investigation widely used in both civil and criminal fields. Employers who observe continuing shortages of cash or merchandise in their stores or factories will use investigators as ropers by hiring them as employees. Employers who want to know the reactions and feelings of employees will employ "ropers" also.

In the realm of police work roping is used extensively in many fields. It is most common in the purchase of illicit or contraband articles such as drugs, alcohol, pornographic literature, or stolen goods. The "roper" has also been widely used as the cellmate of a suspect from whom admissions or confessions are often extracted by the new "buddy."

In every phase of observation there is one word that must forever be in the investigator's mind—patience—and more patience. It becomes extremely trying for an energetic investigator to be relegated to a waiting or walking assignment. But because the tempo of the investigation on a shadowing detail is not set by the investigator but by the subject, the investigator has no alternative but to conform with the pace set.

There is a story about a probationary Secret Service operative who reported one morning to the New York office for his first day's duty. The probationary operative's chief called him into his office and gave him his first assignment. The probationer was instructed to be outside the Woolworth Building at 10 A.M. that very morning, at which time a tall man wearing a derby hat and a gray suit with a pink carnation in the lapel would come out of these premises. The operative was instructed to follow this subject continually until 5 P.M., at which time the tail would cease. He was to take no action other than to note all movements and activity of the subject and, if possible, he was not to lose sight of the man he was following.

Promptly at 10 A.M. the tall man, wearing derby, gray suit, and pink carnation came out of the swinging doors of the Woolworth Building. After a brief pause, he started walking uptown on Broadway, the Secret Service operative intently on his tail. The subject kept walking and walking until he reached the corner of 138th Street and St. Ann's Avenue in the Bronx, approximately seven miles from the starting point. He entered a restaurant located on this corner, sat down, and ordered some food. The exhausted probationer also entered the restaurant, and while his throbbing feet rested a bit, he also ordered some food.

After some thirty minutes, the suspect arose from his table, paid his check, and left the restaurant. The operative followed. The subject stopped on the sidewalk to light a cigar, then turned downtown again and walked all the way back to the Woolworth Building, reaching that place about 3 P.M. The operative faithfully panted after him, his patent leather shoes now breaking at the seams. His feet were beyond hurting. The subject entered a tobacco shop in the Woolworth Building, bought some cigars, lighted one, and started walking back uptown toward the Bronx.

This was too much! The exhausted, exasperated probationer hurried up to the suspect and almost shouted, "Here's a nickel, you S.O.B. If you are going to the Bronx again, take the subway."

The next morning the probationer was told he was no longer on Uncle Sam's payroll. He was fired for becoming impatient and losing his head. The suspect was apparently a "plant." Whether the story is true or not doesn't matter. The necessity for immeasurable patience and coolness does matter.

Observation and its allied activities are most frequently employed in obtaining the necessary evidence to show that a person suspected of committing a particular act is in fact the perpetrator of the deed. The converse is also true in that a suspect may be absolved of suspicion.

Employers or executives may obtain numerous anonymous complaints about the conduct of their employees. The complaints may savor of actual dishonesty, or they may cast reflection on the integrity or loyalty of the employee. The communications may cast aspersions on the personal life of the subject which, if true, might reflect seriously on the organization employing him. The executive cannot operate his activity efficiently unless he verifies or negates the truth of the accusation. In many cases a loyal employee, an associate, or even his wife may be the subject of an unjust accusation based on personal malice. If the subject were confronted with the accusation, tension and bad feeling might be created. Discreet and efficient shadowing will often disclose the falsity of the accusation without the suspect being aware he is the subject of accusation and an ensuing investigation. On the other hand, if proper observation discloses the truth of the allegation contained in the complaint, the investigation is well justified. The point is, however, that all complaints must ordinarily be investigated, and proper observation will not create a rift between the subject and the principal if the complaint is proved to be unfounded.

In any type of shadowing or observation, the exigencies

created by the particular situation are so varied that the investigator's native ingenuity should be his chief guide. Rules of conduct are generally formulated on the spot to meet the particular emergency.

There are certain basic rules, however, which all investigators should know and employ when necessary.

When a subject is being tailed in an automobile, the importance of the case will determine the number of investigators needed. There may be as many as three or four. The subject's automobile will be followed at a discreet distance by the car containing the first investigator. The other investigators will follow, but by prearrangement they will replace one another behind the car being followed so that the subject will not be alarmed by having the same car behind him for a long period.

If a number of investigators are not available simultaneously, it is wise, especially on a loose tail, for the investigator to alternate automobiles each day. An automobile rental agency can serve this purpose.

At night it is easier for one car to maintain a tail. The investigator conducting this type of night activity should occasionally pass the subject of the investigation on a clear road. Some investigators have a special switch installed on their dashboards permitting the extinguishing of either one or both of the tail lights without affecting the headlights. By this subterfuge, it will appear that a car with one tail light passed the suspect the first time, a car with two tail lights the second time, and a car with no tail lights at the third passing. It is possible also to install lenses in the tail light with dashboard control which may show the lights red or colorless. The investigator should remember when driving without lights or when the tail lights are switched off that his foot brake will cause a light to flash when applied. Proper adjustment in advance will rectify this giveaway.

If it becomes necessary for the investigator to use a taxicab to tail another taxi, the driver should be instructed to continue some distance beyond the destination of the first car. In most places cab drivers must make reports of each fare indicating the place of pickup and destination. It may not be advisable to have such a report on record. The investigator should avoid using a taxicab to tail a private car whenever possible because the cab driver may communicate with the owner of the private car by using the registration number of the tailed car.

If the investigator's car is parked at night in a vantage point for observation purposes, it is advisable for him to sit in the back seat where he will be less noticeable. The automobile should be parked in a shadowed area if possible.

It is advisable for the investigator to wear dark clothes for any type of night shadowing unless operating in a place where fashion dictates light clothes. A man in a dark felt hat and black suit would be just as out of place on Flagler Street, Miami, in February as would be a man in a white linen suit and panama hat in Times Square, New York, the same night. On any type of shadowing detail, the investigator should have both a cap and a hat in his car. Switching headgear and occasionally driving without head-covering will create the illusion of different persons being at the wheel of the car. On tail jobs it is recommended that the investigator who does not wear eyeglasses ordinarily carry a pair with him and don them on occasion.

Disguises of theatrical or Sherlock Holmes type are not advised. They will often invite attention because of imperfections. Proper disguises can be applied only by make-up artists, and they are not ordinarily available to the average investigator.

A clever contrivance has been developed by a number of investigators who are mechanically inclined. Anyone can make one, and nothing like this instrument is on the market. It is of invaluable assistance in an automobile tail.

The investigator makes a rough radio sending set with the

aid of any radio repairman by attaching a small dry-cell battery to a vacuum tube. The entire mechanism fits into a cigar box. The tube issues a shriek or howl similar to the interference noises sometimes heard on a radio. This sound can be detected, of course, only by another radio receiving set in the vicinity.

The investigator waits for an auspicious time when he can be undetected and attaches the contrivance to the axle or other unnoticeable protuberance on the subject's automobile. When the subject drives away, the investigator follows at a distance varying from one half to one mile.

The investigator should have a colleague with a small receiving set and a loop antenna in the car. The shriek set up by the vacuum tube in the subject's car will be picked up at full strength by the loop antenna. When the noise vanishes suddenly it means that the subject car has made a turn. A rapid manipulation of the loop antenna until the noise is picked up will disclose the course of the turn. If the first car picks up speed and lengthens the distance between the cars there will be no vanishing of the howl, merely a slow diminution. The tailing investigator can always keep track of the subject at a safe distance by means of the simple directional finder.

In automobile tailing it is of paramount importance that the vehicle used by the investigator should be unobtrusive and of standard make. Unusual accoutrements or accessories or a brilliant paint job will serve the same negative purpose as a siren. They will be a giveaway.

Sometimes the investigator will have the tables turned on him, and he will find himself tailed by the suspicious suspect. If the investigator believes he is being tailed, he should drive around the block several times, noting the traffic in his rear vision mirror. If an available dead-end street is known to the investigator he should drive in and see if he is followed.

Often it will be found practicable, when a subject is suspected of making lengthy trips at stated intervals, to tail him only part way each trip, picking up the tail at the place where it was terminated previously.

There are times when the investigator may desire to signal an associate in such a way as not to attract undue attention. This is difficult, especially at night. It must be realized that the subject of the investigation may know that he is "hot" and therefore is alert to any form of unusual manifestation. The usual methods of acknowledgments, such as blinking lights, waving, and calling are discouraged. A safe way of signaling is lighting a match. The match used should be an ordinary wooden one with phosphorous head, not the safety type from a matchbook. The upper half of the match should be rolled in melted wax. Candle drippings are ideal for this purpose. The match then becomes waterproof. If the investigator is out in the rain for hours he can always procure an instantaneous light, even by scratching the match on a wet surface. In addition to the fact that the flame of a wooden match is larger than that of a safety match, the wax will treble the flame and for a brief moment neither the rain nor the wind will extinguish the blaze. Every investigator should have a supply of such matches. When the match is ignited a cigar or cigaret should always be lighted to carry through the fiction.

When an operative is engaged in a foot tail, he should shift from left to right and not remain directly behind the subject. If the subject window-shops, the investigator should stop behind him, and if the subject repeats this performance, the investigator may pass him if the corner of the street is some distance away. A two- or three-man tail may be conducted on foot in the same general manner as in automobiles. It is easier to tail on foot (but hard on the feet!) because the investigators may use both sides of the street in keeping the suspect under observation.

If the tail takes place in the summer when hats are not being worn, the investigator should carry a cap or soft felt hat rolled up in his pocket and use it occasionally. A coat or jacket should be alternately worn and carried. Glasses should also be alternately worn and removed. The investigator should avoid smoking a pipe on a tail. Many investigators are "made" because the pipe-smoking man stands out more than the cigaret smoker. Carrying a cane should also be avoided. In brief, the investigator should be unobtrusive and effacing in clothes and demeanor on a tailing assignment and he should do nothing and wear nothing to invite attention.

If the investigator must "wait his detail out" in a hotel lobby, theater waiting room, railroad station, or any other public waiting place, he should endeavor to obtain a seat with the light behind him and in such a location as to observe all points of entrance and egress. Sitting with the light coming from behind should be a common practice for all investigators in every field of activity. In addition to placing the investigator in an unobtrusive background, the subject of the investigation is brought out more clearly. If the investigator feels the subject knows of the tail, he should be on the alert for uncommon means of egress in public buildings and hotels such as service exits, garage exits, fire exits, employee exits, and basement exits.

On an automobile tail the investigator may sometimes find it necessary to go through a red stop light in traffic or to violate speed laws to keep up with the subject. If stopped by a traffic officer, the investigator can usually continue on his way after a brief diplomatic explanation and display of credentials. A strong fraternal feeling exists between investigative agents and enforcement agents, based on a knowledge and respect for each others' problems. The fledgling investigator should foster and maintain this feeling.

In shadowing, as in every phase of investigation, it is the minor details which should be noticed. The suspect or criminal will usually plan the basic pattern of his scheme, but he is prone to overlook minor details which, to the trained investigator, become signposts. No detail however minute or seemingly trivial should be overlooked by the investigator. Many a troublesome problem has been solved by the minute scrutiny of scraps of paper found in a suspect's wastepaper basket. The aid of a co-operative maid or porter in a hotel has been frequently enlisted in placing new blotters in the room of the suspect in the hope of subsequently being able to decipher the data written and blotted.

The investigator will find there is no substitute for experience. When not on actual assignment, the investigator should practice shadowing or tailing in order to get the feel of such work. It is easy, when driving a car, to see how long a strange car can be kept in sight. When out for a stroll, it becomes an interesting game to see how far a pedestrian can be followed undetected. If the pedestrian realizes he is being followed, nothing is lost.

The investigator should always be alert for new methods and procedures. This applies not only to observation but to the entire field of investigation. Complacency and self-satisfaction have no place in the investigator's life. He should always discuss the latest techniques with other investigators, and he should be ready to pick up and adopt a new quirk that has been tried successfully by a colleague. On the same premise, he should be willing to share his knowledge with others in the profession.

No good investigator depends solely on the conventional, tried methods employed in his field. He should be fearless about improvising new methods of assault upon novel problems presented. The manner of solution devised by the courageous investigator may be so new as to defy ordinary modes of procedure, but he should remember that the heresy of today is the orthodoxy of tomorrow.

The good investigator should familiarize himself with the haunts and habits of an important subject so that he will know where to locate him. He should know if the subject likes herring or blintzes or steak or fish. He should also know if he is a music lover or a poolroom or race-track addict. Any information of this kind will be found helpful in relocating a lost subject.

A clever criminal was caught by a patient investigator masquerading as a scrubman, actually wielding a mop in a railroad station for almost two months. The suspect in this case would check a parcel in one of the automatic checking lockers. Several hours later he would take his parcel out, but in the meantime he had made a duplicate of the key. He did this in a number of public places in the city having the locker service until he had almost one hundred keys in his possession fitting various check boxes all over the city. He would do some shadowing himself, and when he saw an expensive-looking package or unusually expensive luggage deposited in a locker, he would lift it in a short time if he had the key to that particular box.

After the method of this suspect became known, the investigator in question arranged for several colleagues to deposit daily in certain checking lockers the finest-looking luggage obtainable. The investigator, in working clothes and with mop and pail, was always within visual distance of the lockers containing the expensive luggage. It was an easy matter to apprehend the violator when he was caught red-handed.

The investigator should develop a feeling of confidence in himself and in his own judgment. Most investigative problems arise in the field, and action must be taken immediately. The investigator may not have time to call his superior for an opinion or to refer to books for a possible solution.

It is a matter of common knowledge that many men employ private investigators to check the background of a prospective son-in-law. In one such case the investigators unearthed information that the prospective bridegroom was a charlatan of the worst sort. Before the report of the investigators was submitted, the anguished client telephoned their office to inform them his daughter had just left with her fiance and they were on their way to a neighboring town to be married. The father did not want his daughter to know he had retained investigators, yet he wanted to apprize her of her fiance's character without relating the source of the information. Time was desperately needed.

Two investigators left town immediately in an automobile, caught up with the couple's car, and tailed it for a short while, trying to decide what their next move should be. The investigator who was driving passed the couple's car and noticed the adventurer was at the wheel. Traffic was proceeding at a good pace when the investigator jammed his brakes in a sudden stop and the adventurer crashed into the rear of the investigator's car. No one was hurt, but the cars were quite badly damaged. A highway patrolman came along almost immediately and the investigator insisted on having the driver of the car that crashed into him arrested, charged with reckless driving, and taken to a nearby court.

In the meantime the distraught father arrived on the scene, the wedding was postponed, and when the investigators' report was completed, the contents of it were conveyed to the daughter and the affair was broken up.

No brief is held for the investigator's deliberate action in creating a dangerous situation. Whether the deliberate sudden stop is ethical is not debated. The facts are related in order to show the originality employed by an investigator to obtain a very essential delay.

One of the most valuable aids to the investigator on a night-shadowing detail is the instrument which is the outgrowth of the sniperscope developed in World War II. By the adaptation of the infrared ray in a tiny image tube—less than two inches in diameter and less than five inches long—the sniperscope enabled an American soldier to hit a target the size of a man at a distance of over two hundred feet. It was also used by drivers of fast army vehicles on dark nights when traveling without lights.

This night fighting aid has now been adapted to civilian use, and modern police agencies and investigators can well use the device on night observation details. The sniperscope outlines in the dark the shadow of an object which would ordinarily be absolutely invisible to the naked eye.

Another instrument developed in World War II which will prove to be of inestimable aid to the investigator is the opto-phone, an ordinary telescope-like device mounted on a tripod, which will flash a seven-mile beam at night and a four-mile beam in the daytime. The use of an infrared filter makes the light invisible to the naked human eye. When the beam is focused on its objective, where the receiving apparatus is located, a still greater marvel of science results. The beam actually transmits the voice of the speaker to its destination without the use of wires.

The good investigator when actively engaged on an important tailing assignment should have a substantial sum of money in his possession at all times to meet any contingency requiring expenditure. The investigator might find it necessary suddenly to check in at an expensive hotel, or to buy a railroad ticket to a distant point, or he might have an opportunity to obtain certain information if he properly cultivated the informant by entertainment or other means. An understanding should be established by the investigator with the principal about such outlays of money.

In certain government bureaus an investigator is allowed a special "pink slip" fund. It is presumed that a man working in an investigative capacity for a government agency is the soul of integrity. Certain men are designated who may spend sums of money with no accounting required. The expenditures may be for the purchase of information with no disclosure of the identity of the seller, or it may be for unusual expenses of other sorts. By filling out a pink slip indicating that the expenditure was necessary in furtherance of an investigation, no further explanation and no additional voucher are required.

The question of expense in conducting an investigation frequently pillages the investigator. This holds true to a greater extent in governmental and municipal bureaus which operate according to set, definite rules concerning allowable expenses. To attain certain ends, the investigator sometimes finds it necessary to make unauthorized expenditures.

A seasoned, conscientious investigator for a government agency was once tailing a suspect on a very rainy day. Both the suspect and the investigator carried umbrellas. A taxicab came to the curb; the suspect closed his umbrella, climbed in the cab, and was driven away. Almost immediately the investigator hailed a taxi to the curb and opened the door to enter it. He turned to close his umbrella but it stuck. In the meantime the suspect's cab was fast disappearing. The investigator abandoned his umbrella on the sidewalk in order to avoid delay and instructed his driver to follow the suspect's cab.

When the investigator submitted his monthly expense account, he inserted the item, "1 umbrella—$3.50." The chief clerk disallowed the item, noting it was not a permissible expense. The following month the investigator inserted the same detail in his expense account, and again it was disallowed. The third month the result was the same.

The fourth month the expense account did not carry the item of the umbrella. When the chief clerk handed the investigator his expense check, he commented he was glad the investigator had finally seen the light and decided to forget the matter of the umbrella. The answer was, "It's in there."

The chief of one of America's largest investigative agencies always engages extra rooms when he goes to a hotel. He takes over the rooms directly above and below and on each side of his own suite and leaves them unoccupied in order that no eavesdropper can be present. He took his cue from top-flight violators. Modern science has made it very easy to detect and record conversations in adjoining rooms or in a room directly underneath or overhead. The use of the wired microphone is almost obsolete, however, because of the difficulty presented in wiring and because the crafty, shady character searches a room thoroughly for evidence of a wired apparatus before he makes it his headquarters.

The development of the vacuum tube has made it possible to place a stethoscope-like microphone against the wall of an adjoining room so that conversations are amplified sufficiently to be heard plainly. If the conversations are to be perpetuated as evidence, recording machines are used to make records of the talks.

In an emergency, if the investigator does not have the proper technical paraphernalia available, he can sometimes overhear a conversation in an adjoining room if he can procure a champagne glass with a hollow stem. The investigator should place the mouth of the glass flush against the wall and the base close to his ear. The glass acts as a direct conductor of the sound.

It is not the purpose of this book to give the technical aspects of all the mechanical means available to investigators. Certain contrivances are available, and their uses will be set forth. Many forms of apparatus are not on the market but can be easily made by a person with some technical knowledge.

Mention was made previously of the one-tube "broadcaster" which set up a howl and of its usefulness in tailing. Some of the largest investigative organizations use a similar contrivance to ascertain the activities of a suspect group.

A broadcasting set tuned in at a certain wave length is hidden in a room, hall, or meeting place where the group under surveillance is to meet. Sufficient power for amplification is present so that the slightest whisper is magnified. The listener or "Supervisor" may be across the street or several blocks away, wherever he can obtain suitable quarters. Often an automobile parked in the neighborhood will suffice as the pickup station. The conversations in the meeting place will all be transmitted over the special wave length and picked up. No wiring of any kind is necessary.

The main problem in using this instrument is to find a place where the broadcasting mechanism, which is noiseless and powered by batteries, can be secreted. There are known instances of the mechanism being placed in the walls or ceiling which were ripped out and repainted. This, of course, is feasible only if sufficient time is available to the investigator to make the proper preparations. There are other instances of the device being secreted in the spaces used by hidden radiators, in toilet-bowl compartments, in the hollows of upright sinks, in couches, and in false dresser compartments. The equipment is expensive, however, and if discovered by the subject can generally be considered lost.

The latest telephone tapping equipment automatically records conversations on discs. It supersedes the ordinary wire cut-in described earlier, which required a "tapper" to use headphones and record what he heard in shorthand.

While on roping or undercover assignments the investigator should divorce himself from his real identity. He should have no credentials on his person and no evidence indicating he is an investigator. He should have nothing on his person or in his room which would reveal his true identity. This means he should use new linens, suits, or other clothing if what he ordinarily wears bears his name or initials. He should discard his hat if it contains his name or initials. He should dispense with all letters and documents on his person addressed to him. All membership cards in clubs or organizations should be discarded. If a maid or other person were to rifle his room or possessions, no clue should be found to indicate he is anyone other than the person he professes to be.

In addition to destroying the old identity, the investigator who is posing as someone other than himself should create the new one. This is done not merely by assuming another name, but by building a fiction and activity about that name. If the investigator registers in a hotel under an assumed name in an undercover capacity, he should have mail sent to him there addressed to the name he is using; he should send himself telegrams; he should have himself paged; he should have C.O.D. purchases delivered to him at the hotel. Some investigators even open a checking account in their assumed name and pay bills by check. The alias which the investigator has assumed should become a living, vital person. There have been instances where investigators have gone to the trouble of having rings, watches, and other jewelry engraved with their new initials. Others actually have gone into temporary business under the assumed name.

The investigator should never telephone his office or an investigative headquarters from his hotel telephone. Switchboard operators keep a record of outgoing calls, and unless the investigator is alert and careful in all his actions he may trip himself while attempting to cover his quarry. Means of communication with the investigator's organization are worked out before he goes on assignment and, needless to say, his organization does not write to him at his base of operations.

Frequently it becomes necessary for the investigator to make guarded inquiries in a disguised voice. There are a number of simple ways to disguise the voice when talking over the telephone. If a handkerchief is placed over the mouthpiece of the instrument there is sufficient change in the voice to make it generally unrecognizable. A piece of crumpled newspaper in the mouthpiece will vary it still further, and a piece of tissue paper crumpled and placed in the mouthpiece will result in a still different voice pitch. In using the old-type telephone instrument (not the present widely used hand set), the mouthpiece may be held closely to the chest. The voice emerges clear and understandable on the other end—but different. If the mouthpiece is lowered from the chest and held closely to the diaphragm, the voice will come out on the receiving end still different, and deeper.

Emphasis cannot be too strongly place on the use of the motion-picture camera for any form of observation. The pictures are the best evidence in a court, and practically incontrovertible as to the facts presented.

Although whenever feasible this instrument should be used, existing technical difficulties are of such a nature as to make it difficult to obtain motion pictures without being observed. The chief difficulties are lighting and the fact that a motion-picture camera is difficult to conceal. One of the best methods by which motion pictures may be taken is by the use of a closed delivery truck. A closed body with a small aperture on each of the four sides allows exposure toward all directions for the camera in the truck, yet conceals both operator and camera.

If the investigator uses this method, it is wise to have the truck marked as if it were a firm's delivery truck to avoid having it regarded with suspicion. The innocent-looking delivery truck has been the means of uncovering many insurance frauds, and has been used frequently for procuring evidence in both civil and criminal cases.

A substitute for the moving-picture camera can be found in the watch camera. While the results are not as effective as a roll of films, they are much easier to obtain. This type of camera is a little larger than an ordinary watch. The winding stem, however, contains a lens, and photographs can be taken by the mere ruse of presumably pulling out a watch and casually winding it, the stem pointing at the object to be photographed.

Various refinements of shadowing and tailing will be developed by the investigator in his respective field. Each field presents certain problems peculiar to it, and they should be studied and developed by its specialized investigators.

Thus the investigator in a rural area should develop a naturalist's keenness and insight. If a woods road does not give the appearance of being used, the sight of oil or grease on the grass, or a broken fresh sapling should indicate immediately the recent passing of an automobile on that road. The investigator in this field should notice barn roofs after a snowstorm, and if part of the roof is bare of snow which has melted, he should take heed. Perhaps the warmth of the animals underneath has created sufficient heat to melt the snow on that part of the roof, but could it be a moonshine still in the barn that gave out the heat? The investigator must get the right answer.

The investigator in New York City should know every foot of the labyrinth of subway systems. He should know fire regulations in order to understand the location of fire exits that could be used by a subject in an effort to shake the tail. He should know exactly how to find a corridor or lavatory room in an office building from which he could take a picture of events in another office building across the street. He must develop a huge fund of special factual knowledge.

CHAPTER SEVEN

EVIDENCE

THE investigator is a fact-finder, but he must know the laws concerning the nature of his activities. He should procure evidence in such a way that the findings can be admitted by a judge, understood by a jury, and remain impregnable to any attack by opposing counsel.

Because of the inherent nature of his work, the investigator should possess a moderate knowledge of jurisprudence. He must have a working knowledge of the laws of evidence and the necessary components of the more common crimes.

The average investigator is in constant contact with various investigative and enforcement agencies, and he should learn to speak their parlance. The investigator must know thoroughly common legal, criminal, and investigative terminology, so that he is accepted into the investigative fraternity.

Evidence is proof of allegations. It may be (a) direct; (b) indirect, which includes circumstantial evidence; or (c) hearsay.

Direct evidence is simply that which the senses perceive. Any fact to which a witness testifies based on what he saw, heard, smelled, touched, or tasted, is direct evidence.

It frequently happens that no witness was present at the commission of an act which is sought to be re-enacted or explained in a courtroom. The necessity of resorting to other means of proof is obvious. Crimes are secret. Most persons engaged in criminal or questionable activities seek the security of secrecy, darkness, and remoteness to cloak their misdeeds. It becomes necessary therefore to use all other available modes of evidence in addition to direct testimony.

Circumstantial evidence is therefore brought into play. It is evidence which seeks to establish a conclusion by inference from proved facts.

As an illustration, assume that a pedestrian walking down the street heard a scream come from a store. Almost immediately he saw a man rush from the store, a bloody knife in his hand. The pedestrian entered the store and found a woman on the floor dead, her throat cut.

In this case the only direct evidence to which the pedestrian could testify would be that he saw a person run from the store holding a bloody knife. He did not see the woman killed, nor could he state positively that the fleeing man was the killer. Yet the prosecutor would seek to establish the conclusion that the man with the knife was the killer by inference from the proved facts which were the events actually witnessed by the pedestrian.

Unfortunately, although circumstantial evidence is admissible for consideration by the jury, many an innocent man has been convicted on such evidence. In the illustration cited, the fleeing man may not have been the killer. He could have been a confused, stunned person who stumbled on the dying woman and in his fright grabbed the knife unthinkingly and ran out. In Professor Edwin M. Borchard's book *Convicting the Innocent* sixty-five cases of actual convictions of persons, later shown to be innocent, are fully detailed. Practically every one of the convictions was obtained on circumstantial evidence. It is a grave responsibility for the jury to consider and evaluate circumstantial evidence.

Admissible evidence is that evidence which a court may properly receive in a trial. Both direct evidence and circumstantial evidence may be admitted as testimony.

The relevancy of testimony must be established before it is admitted into evidence. Anything tending to prove or disprove the issue is logically relevant. No evidence is admissible unless it is relevant. Evidence is irrelevant if it is not applicable to the issues joined. In other words, evidence is irrelevant and therefore inadmissible when it does not tend to establish or create a belief about the existence or non-existence of facts in issue. To be relevant, the evidence must be material, and it must have an effective bearing on the question in issue. The test of materiality is whether or not the evidence tends to establish or clarify controversial fact.

Hearsay evidence is a statement made by a witness on the authority of another, and not from personal knowledge or observation. Hearsay evidence is inadmissible with certain well-defined exceptions.

Some of the more common exceptions to the rules of exclusion generally applicable to hearsay evidence are declarations against interest, dying declarations, res gestae, reputation, public records, and statements made at a prior time.

A dying declaration usually is the declaration of a person who was the victim of a homicidal attack. It must be made by the victim when he is actually *in extremis* and dying, and he must know he is dying. The declarant must have actually died before the witness to whom the declaration was made can testify to it.

Declarations are admitted in evidence under the res gestae theory when they are uttered at the time of the event in issue and as a part of the act or happening, or so close to it in point of time as to preclude the fabrication of a story. The test is whether or not the declaration is shown to have been uttered spontaneously or contemporaneously with the event.

A simple example is that of the motorman of a trolley car who cried, "My God! I have no brakes," just as his car crashed into a truck.

A person's character is established by his general reputation, and testimony is allowed on behalf of a defendant to show his reputation in a community.

Public documents when otherwise competent are admissible as evidence of the facts contained therein, without the testimony of the officer who made the record. This exception to the hearsay rules rests on the great inconvenience that might result in compelling the attendance of the official. The writer of the documents might be removed from office or dead at the time of the trial, but the entries are admissible because they were made in the public interest by a person officially performing his duties.

Testimony given by a witness at a trial is admissible in any subsequent action or proceeding when the litigants and the issues are the same as in the prior trial and when the witness has since died or has become incompetent to testify because he is insane or is out of the jurisdiction.

The common-law restrictions on the witnesses have been removed generally by statute in all states in the country. At common law one who had no religious belief or was a convicted criminal, an interested party, or an insane person was deemed incompetent to testify.

Under present laws, a felon may be a witness; a husband and wife are legally competent in certain instances to testify against each other; and interested persons may testify. The test as to whether or not a witness is competent is whether or not he understands the nature of an oath, and can tell a comprehensible story. All testimony must be under oath, even that of children and the mentally defective. A person mentally defective is not barred from testifying if he understands the obligation of an oath and is capable of giving a correct account of the matters in issue. The same rule applies to a child whose competency depends on intelligence, judgment, and understanding, and not on age. The jury, of course, weighs the testimony in the light of the impressions it receives as to the credibility and stability of the witness.

Every witness is subject to the right of cross examination. This method is universally recognized as the most efficacious test for the discovery of truth. One of the reasons for generally excluding hearsay testimony is because the declarant whose statements are offered by another cannot be subjected to the test of cross-examination. The right to cross-examine a witness does not have to be exercised, and the witness may leave the stand without being subjected to cross-examination.

Cross-examination of a single witness may sometimes take days until the truth is elicited. Frequently, however, a shifty witness, who is not too intelligent or who displays fear or nervousness, may be subtly guided into revealing the truth quickly.

An actual case which has been the subject of many anecdotes illustrates this point. A plaintiff who claimed partial paralysis as a result of an accident insisted that he was unable to raise either hand higher than his head. While some injuries had been incurred by the plaintiff, counsel for the defendant felt that they were purposely being exaggerated. After the plaintiff had completed his testimony, the first question the opposing counsel asked him on cross examination was, "Show with your right hand how far you could raise it before you had the accident." The plaintiff immediately raised his right hand in a straight line over his head. The clever investigator and the clever lawyer must be on the alert for such opportunities and they will then know where pressure is to be applied.

The investigator who is instrumental in building up the evidence for action by his principal should play an active part at the trial in suggesting methods of procedure to the trial counsel, especially with reference to the dependability and intelligence of certain witnesses and the order in which they should be called. The investigator should also review the testi-

mony before the trial with the witnesses he has previously interviewed. This review will act as a memory refresher for the
potential witness. Care should be exercised, however, that the
review does not become a coaching session whereby the investigator advises the witness what to say.

When the investigator renews his contacts with his witnesses
in the courtroom or just prior to the trial, he should always
ask the prospective witness to pick out the subject of his pro-
posed testimony if that person is in the courtroom. Very often
a trial may take place two or three years after the happening of
the occurrence which is the basis for the litigation. A witness
may remember specifically the nature of the events that he
witnessed but he may not remember the face of the other
person or persons involved.

The interested party usually sits near his attorney and co-
operates with him in the presentation of the case. Many a
clever lawyer, however, has won his case where identification
was a determining factor by having someone other than the
interested party sit next to him during the course of the trial.
The attorney would convey the impression that this person
was his client by his actions and continuing consultations with
him. In such cases, when the witness is cross-examined and
asked to indicate the person in the courtroom who is the subject of his testimony, he may frequently indicate the person by
the lawyer's side. Previous identification by the witness of the
subject of his testimony will eliminate the possibility of this
mistake, which might easily create a serious doubt in the minds
of the jury as to the dependability of the entire testimony of
the witness.

Under certain circumstances it may be advisable for one
witness to be excluded from the courtroom during the testimony of another. The request to separate witnesses will generally be granted by the court, if made in good faith and in an
honest attempt to avoid fraud or collusion. It should be re-

membered, however, that a party to the action may not be excluded from the courtroom.

Certain facts sought to be introduced into evidence need not be proved. These are facts which the court is charged with in taking judicial notice, which is the knowledge a judge will officially take of a fact without proof. No fixed rule can be laid down establishing what will be judicially noticed. Courts will notice the facts which are a part of the general knowledge of the country and such facts are ever-changing and never static.

A state court will take judicial notice of the statutes of its own state, and all courts judicially know the Constitution of the United States and the Acts of Congress.

Judges generally will take judicial notice of matters of arts and science which are generally recognized and should be known to men of average intelligence. For instance, a court will take judicial notice that a compass needle points north and that the normal period of human gestation is two hundred and eighty days. Other matters of common knowledge such as the kicking propensities of a mule, the ability of a duck to swim, and the scratching habit of cats have been the subjects of judicial notice.

Certain communications are privileged because of the inherent confidential relationship which inspired them. The parties to such privileged communications are, under certain circumstances, made incompetent by law to testify to such communications. The four confidential relationships that fall within this category are: (1) attorney and client; (2) clergyman and penitent; (3) physician and patient; and (4) husband and wife. In the case of attorney and client, the privilege is strictly the client's, and it may be waived by him.

In most states the privileged relationship between patient and doctor exists only if the doctor has been consulted in a professional capacity for advice or treatment. The privilege is the patient's and may be waived by him. Certain exceptions to this rule have been formulated by statutes in many states compelling the physician to disclose gunshot wounds suffered by a patient whom he treats.

At common law, neither spouse could at one time testify against the other. The statutes adopted by the various states have modified the common-law rule so that under certain conditions, which vary in the different states, testimony by one spouse against the other is allowable. Confidential communications between husband and wife are still recognized generally as privileged from disclosure without the consent of both.

While minor abrogations exist, the basic rule is unchanged that a confession or admission made to a clegyman, while the latter is acting in his clerical capacity, is a privileged communication.

The investigator should particularly remember a peculiar quirk to the privileged communications ruling. If a third party overhears a conversation between any of the privileged parties, most jurisdictions allow the third party to testify what he overheard. The privilege of the client, patient, penitent, or spouse does not apply to the one who overhears.

Properly authenticated photographs are admissible in evidence whenever they are competent to describe a person, place, or object. The investigator should have photographs taken whenever necessary. The photographs are properly authenticated by the testimony of any person familiar with the subject matter portrayed. He must state it is a true representation or likeness of the person, place, or object sought to be described.

Diagrams, maps, and sketches are also admitted into evidence in connection with the testimony of witnesses who have testified to their correctness. Photographs, maps, diagrams, or sketches should be made at the scene of the incident as soon as possible after the time the event occurs. Visual evidence of any sort has great psychological effect on a jury which takes the exhibits into the jury room to ponder over them at leisure. The exhibits often serve to keep fresh in the minds of the jury testimony that might have been forgotten.

In taking a photograph of an object, or the scene of an occurrence, with the intention of using this photograph subsequently at a trial, care should be exercised to insure that the scene or object photographed remain unchanged from its condition at the time of the occurrence to the time the photograph was taken. If it is necessary to chalk off or otherwise specially identify a part of a scene, two photographs should be taken, one of the scene before any chalk markings were made, and one of the scene with the markings. A photograph with markings or inscriptions may be objected to by an alert attorney as not truly portraying the scene it is supposed to represent.

Exhibits of any sort should not be tampered with, and they should be maintained as near their original state as possible for the time of trial. Care should be taken that all exhibits are labeled and sufficiently identified by each investigator possessing them to show a continuous chain of custody from the time of the occurrence to the time it is sought to be introduced into evidence. If the chain of custody is broken, objection to its introduction may be made on the ground that it may have been tampered with and that there is no absolute proof that the exhibit is exactly what it purports to be.

In addition to direct, indirect, and hearsay evidence, there is still another mode of submitting evidence, and this latter method of evidencing a fact is known as "real evidence," the presentation of the object itself, to which the testimony refers, for personal observation by the court and jury. Such objects, when it is convenient, are brought into the courtroom, although occasionally the jury is permitted to go out to inspect an object or a scene not capable of being produced in the courtroom. Evidence thus acquired by self-observation is real or tangible evidence, and it presents the most satisfactory and natural proof.

Most state courts rule that evidence such as books, papers, or other evidential proof which have been unlawfully obtained or seized illegally in violation of the Fourth Amendment to the Constitution, which provides against unlawful search and seizure, may still be admitted. In the federal courts, however, documents or other articles illegally seized by federal agents may not be used as evidence.

In civil actions a plaintiff ordinarily has the right to exhibit his disability or injuries to the court and jury. In certain instances when the matter appears exhibitionistic, the display of certain evidence tending to excite the sympathies of the jury will be barred by the judge. For instance, a plaintiff whose arm was amputated as a result of an accident may not introduce in evidence the severed member preserved in a glass container. The judge has wide latitude in such matters in deciding when the witness is abusing the privilege of exhibiting his personal injuries.

The investigator who is assisting at a trial should be on the alert for any untoward action on the part of any of the jurors, such for instance as an unauthorized inspection of premises sought to be described in court. All evidence in a trial must be furnished to the entire jury in open court and extraneous action of almost any sort on the part of a juror is improper.

The receiver or hearer of a telephone message may testify to the conversation provided the person with whom the conversation was held could be identified. If the witness knows the speaker and can state that he recognized the speaker's voice, the evidence as to the conversation is admissible.

When the subject matter of testimony is of such technical nature that the proper conclusions to be drawn from the facts depend on professional or scientific knowledge or skill, qualified experts may express their opinions as to the proper inference to be drawn from a given set of facts as an aid to the jury in reaching its own conclusions. The expert must be first qualified as such before he can testify. While a basic qualification to act as an expert in a particular field is necessary, extraordinary qualifications may sway the jury. The testimony of the ordinary expert and the testimony of the extraordinary, nationally known expert are equally admissible. The jury may use different means of evaluation, however, based on the comparative fame and skill of the witnesses as brought out by their qualifications. The field of investigation is so diversified that the active investigator will constantly find himself soliciting the opinions of expert witnesses and using them to obtain the full measure of proof necessary in establishing a clear-cut determination of the facts in issue.

Writings offered for testimony are in general divided into two classes, public and private documents. The former consist of records made by public officers while in the performance of their duties. All other writings are private documents.

When public documents are sought to be admitted into evidence, they must be properly authenticated in conformity with the rules of the jurisdiction. Authentication may be effected by certification or exemplification of the document.

Before a private document may be accepted in evidence, the party offering it must prove that it was executed by the person who is declared to have done so.

No proof of the document's execution need be submitted, however, in the following instances: (a) if its genuineness is admitted by the adverse party; (b) if it has been acknowledged in the manner required for the recording of a deed; (c) if the writing is an ancient document which requires proof that the instrument is more than thirty years old.

The prevalent practice followed in most of the courts allows the use of papers for the purpose of refreshing witnesses' recollections if the notes were made contemporaneously with the occurrence or nearly so. It is not required that such a document be introduced in evidence. Some jurisdictions permit the use of any paper whatsoever to refresh the recollection of the witness. In the latter case, however, the weight attached to the testimony of the witness will be diminished if it is brought out on cross-examination that the notes were written at a time remote from the actual occurrence.

Documents not required by law to be attested may be proved by any of the signers or by a person who was present at the time and saw the party affix his signature.

Proof of the handwriting of one of the alleged signers of a document may be submitted by a witness who can prove he has sufficient knowledge of the handwriting of the person in question. It may also be proved by a comparison of the disputed document with the conceded or genuine handwriting. Such comparisons may be made by the expert witness, usually the handwriting expert, or by the jury itself.

The credibility of a witness may be impeached on the following grounds: (a) by showing his generally bad reputation for veracity; (b) by questioning him on cross-examination concerning any immoral, vicious, or criminal acts allegedly committed by him, which may affect his character and tend to show he is not worthy of belief; (c) by showing his bias in favor of the party calling him, his hostility toward the party against whom his testimony is directed, and his interest in the case; (d) by showing that he has been convicted of a crime; (e) by showing that either at the time of the occurrence to which he has testified, or at the time of giving the testimony, he was under the influence of drugs or liquor or was mentally unbalanced.

The investigator is very frequently called upon to establish many of the foregoing facts concerning an important witness who is about to testify for the adversary. The attorney presenting the case in which the investigator is interested will thus have valuable ammunition to counteract the effect of the testimony that may be adduced by the adversary's witness.

The investigator should ascertain, if possible, the relationship of the witness to the interested party on whose behalf he is testifying, his interest in the results of the case, and whether or not he is being paid for testifying. Persons should be interrogated who may know the general reputation of the witness for veracity, and they may possibly be used as impeaching witnesses. Specific instances of vicious, immoral or criminal conduct may be used on cross-examination in an effort to destroy the credibility of the witness.

The business, occupation, or other activities of the witness should be investigated to determine if he is engaged in a nefarious although not necessarily criminal line of work. Thus, if it is determined by investigation that a witness is a bookmaker, or a professional gambler or better, his credibility may be impaired if these facts are brought out on cross-examination.

A witness may be impeached by showing that he has been convicted of a crime. An arrest or indictment may not be shown because these are based upon nothing more than accusations. The witness may not be asked if he has been arrested or tried for a crime. Nothing less than the actual conviction will suffice for impeachment.

If the investigator has reason to suspect that the witness is mentally deranged, or a habitual drunkard, he should leave no stone unturned in his investigation to determine if the witness was under the influence of liquor or drugs, or was mentally unbalanced either at the time of the occurrence to which he testified or at the time of the trial.

The credibility of one's own witness cannot ordinarily be impeached except by the adversary. This is based on the theory of law: "When a party offers a witness in proof of his cause, he thereby in general represents him as worthy of belief."

Nothing can thus ordinarily be done to impugn the credibility of one's own witness by showing his hostility, bias, inconsistency, or that he is a person unworthy of belief.

While a party may not discredit his own witness by showing his prior contradictory statements, he may, if surprised by the testimony, question the witness with respect to previous statements made which are inconsistent with the present testimony, for the technical purpose of refreshing or probing the memory of the witness, and in order to give him an opportunity to explain the apparent inconsistencies. This technical fiction allows a probing of the undependable witness's mind. If the witness, however, should deny having made the prior statement which is inconsistent with his current testimony, his prior statement cannot be proved by other witnesses, because this procedure in effect would be an impeachment by a direct attack on the credibility of the witness.

CHAPTER EIGHT

CRIMES

EVERY investigator, whether engaged in the civil or the criminal phase of investigation, must have a thorough knowledge of those crimes relating to his particular field.

By far the largest percentage of all investigations embrace or contemplate some form of crime or violation, actual or potential, within the scope of its activities.

Crimes are generally divided into the subdivisions of felonies and misdemeanors. The statutes of the several states usually define and segregate the specific crimes described as either felonies or misdemeanors. The felonies are generally classed as the most serious and more heinous crimes, indictable and punished by severe penalties. The misdemeanors are lesser violations.

The federal courts have jurisdiction of those crimes which violate any of the laws of Congress or any United States regulations or statutes. State courts have jurisdiction of crimes committed within their precincts when state laws are violated.

The Constitution of the United States provides that "no person shall be subject for the same offense to be twice put in jeopardy of life or limb." This means that no person can be subjected to a second prosecution for a crime for which he has been tried and duly convicted or acquitted. But a defendant may generally be tried by both a federal court and a state court for the identical offense if statutes of both the state and the federal government were violated by the specific crime. This is not considered double jeopardy. For instance, if a person is caught with a load of untaxed potable alcohol, just out of an illicit still, he may be prosecuted by the federal government for violation of the United States Revenue Laws, and the state in which he was apprehended may prosecute him also for violation of its laws controlling alcoholic beverages.

An arrest is the taking of a person into custody to be held to answer for a crime, and it is made by the actual restraint of the person or by his submission to custody.

A peace officer generally has the right to make an arrest without a warrant for a crime committed in his presence; when the person arrested has committed a felony although not in his presence; or when a felony has actually been committed and there is reasonable cause to believe the person to be arrested has committed it.

In most jurisdictions a private person has the right to arrest a person without a warrant if the person has attempted or committed a crime in his presence.

A complaint, or an information as it is sometimes called, is the allegation made to a judge, magistrate, commissioner, or other proper official, stating that a person is guilty of some designated crime. If sufficient facts appear in the complaint tending to establish the commission of a crime, the official to whom it is submitted will issue a warrant for the arrest of the person charged with it. The warrant must be directed to and executed by a peace officer. A private person may not execute a warrant of arrest, although he may be called upon to aid the peace officer in its execution. In the federal courts either United States commissioners or federal judges issue warrants of arrest to United States marshals for execution.

The information or complaint made to the proper official issuing the warrant may be lodged by either a peace officer or a private person. Investigators are often called upon to file complaints in order to obtain warrants.

An indictment is an accusation in writing, presented by a grand jury to a court, formally charging a person with committing a crime. The grand jury itself is a body of men, varying in number from twelve to twenty-four, whose duty it is after hearing evidence against a defendant to decide whether a sufficient case has been made out against him to warrant holding the accused for trial by an ordinary or petit jury.

The grand jury may hear the investigator's testimony, and if it is deemed sufficient to indicate the commission of a crime by the accused, an indictment will be voted. This indictment is the accusation of the grand jury, which has adopted the charges of the complaining witness for its own. A warrant of arrest is issued upon the indictment, and the defendant is apprehended and held for trial.

It is wise for the investigator to remember this procedure thoroughly and to avail himself of the use of the grand jury to effectuate an arrest whenever feasible, rather than to engage in the practice of signing informations or complaints. The all-important reason for this suggestion lies in the fact that investigative officers are often made the subjects of suits for false arrest if they have been instrumental in effecting the arrest of persons who were later acquitted of the charges made by the investigator and it is found that the investigator did not have sufficient probable cause.

If the investigator withholds his action until he appears before the grand jury, however, he cannot be made a defendant in a suit for false arrest because of any statements made by him to this body. When the investigator testifies before the grand jury, it is solely up to this body to determine the weight or credence it chooses to give to the evidence received. The grand jury may not consider the evidence sufficient to warrant an indictment. On the other hand, if the indictment is voted, it becomes the formal charge which the grand jury makes against the defendant. The investigator who has testified before the grand jury loses his status as an accuser, and in effect the grand jury becomes the accuser.

While it is not intended to burden the reader with involved legal Latin or technical phraseology in this simple discourse on some of the more common crimes, there are nevertheless certain terminologies subject to such common usage that for the investigator not to know them is a serious handicap.

Evidence of corpus delicti must always be present in order to effect a legal conviction. Corpus delicti is the body of the offense, the commission of which must be established before the accused can be legally convicted. An accused cannot be convicted legally upon his unsupported confession. A court cannot consider the confession of an accused as evidence against him unless there be in the record other evidence, either direct or circumstantial, showing the offense charged has been committed. In other words, there must be evidence of the corpus delicti other than the confession itself.

The evidence of corpus delicti need not be sufficient of itself to convince beyond reasonable doubt that the offense charged has been committed, or to cover every element of the charge, or to connect the accused with it. Evidence of the actual crime, no matter how slight, must be shown. For instance, if a man walked into a police station and confessed that he had knifed a man the previous night on a dark street, no conviction could be obtained if the police had no report of the incident and if they could not find the victim.

This theory of law has its roots in the abuses prevalent in medieval times when a man was placed on the rack and tortured into confessing to a crime that he never committed and which in fact never had been committed. The liberalizations of modern law therefore make a legal conviction impossible on confession alone unless there is present some independent segmentary evidence of the crime.

Habeas corpus means literally that "you have the body." It

is a writ issued by the court to bring the person seeking the benefit of it before the courts or judge to determine whether or not he is illegally detained. It is a summary remedy for unlawful restraint of liberty. If an arrested person is held arbitrarily without hearing, he has the right to apply for a writ of *habeas corpus* which compels his jailer or keeper to produce him before the judge for determination of the legality of the restraint.

Prosecutions for all felonies, with the exception of murder, have limitations of time pursuant to which indictments must be found within the prescribed period or future prosecutions are barred. The periods for the various crimes vary in the different states, but the rule is general that the Statute of Limitations does not operate in favor of a defendant while he is out of the state, but lapses during the period he is out of the jurisdiction and begins operating the moment he returns.

There are many presumptions in law, but the most important one for the investigator to remember is that a defendant in a criminal action is presumed to be innocent until proved guilty. If there is a reasonable doubt that guilt is satisfactorily shown, the defendant is entitled to an acquittal. Reasonable doubt has been defined, not as a mere guess or surmise that a man may not be guilty; it is a doubt which a reasonable man would entertain after a fair review of the evidence—a doubt created by the evidence itself. When such a doubt is found, the accused should be acquitted.

A defendant in a criminal action may testify as a witness in his own behalf, but his refusal to take the witness stand and testify does not create any presumption against him.

A confession of a defendant, whether obtained in the course of the judicial proceeding or by the investigator, may be entered in evidence against the defendant unless it was made under the influence of fear, intimidation, threats, or duress of any kind. There must be absolutely no indication that the confession was anything other than a free and voluntary statement.

The good investigator will conduct a careful investigation and will obtain those facts consistent with the guilt of the defendant and inconsistent with his innocence. Confronting the defendant with implicating facts will often result in a confession, making unnecessary the onerous task of proving many allegations.

The investigator must keep in mind the psychological importance of the confession. The amount of proof necessary to convince a jury is greater than the amount necessary to convince the investigator. While the investigator must conduct his investigation in a purely impartial vein, his very interest in the matter investigated lends that subconscious modicum of feeling which makes him prejudiced to some degree, whether he realizes this fact or not. For that reason the investigator in a criminal case should strive for just a little more than he deems enough. The voluntary confession becomes the clincher.

Common law is that system of law which does not rest for its authority upon any express statutes, but derives its force and authority from universal consent and immemorial usage. It prevails except when abrogated by statute, which is the law promulgated by legislative lawmaking bodies such as the Congress and state legislatures.

For example, a common-law marriage is an agreement between a man and a woman to enter into the marriage relationship without ecclesiastical or civil ceremony. In those states which permit common-law marriages, this relationship is perfectly legal if both parties were free to marry, which means if there were no legal impediment to a ceremonial marriage, such as miscegenation, lack of age, incestuous relationship, or a living undivorced spouse.

In those states, however, which abrogated the common-law rule pertaining to marriages, statutes were formulated making it mandatory that a license be issued and a civil or ecclesiastical ceremony be performed. If no statute had been passed on this subject, the common-law rule pertaining to marriages would have prevailed.

The term *venue* means the locality in which an act is done, or where a cause of action arises and from which place the jury is picked to hear the evidence in the trial of the case. Crimes must be tried in the venue where they were committed, although changes of venue will be granted from one county to another in the same state if it can be shown that the defendant cannot receive a fair and impartial trial in the county where the cause of action arose.

In conspiracy cases, the trial can be held in any place where one of the overt acts in the conspiracy was committed. Conspiracy is a continuing crime, and it reaches to every point where any act has been committed in furtherance of the illegal agreement. For this reason, the court in any district where an overt act is committed may try the entire conspiracy. Further data on the elements of conspiracy appear later in this chapter.

If it is necessary to demand the surrender of a defendant by one state or country to another for trial because of a crime committed in the latter jurisdiction, it is effected by the process of extradition. The Constitution provides for extradition from one state to another, and treaty arrangements with other countries govern the procedure when extradition is necessary in such instances.

Coupled with most crimes which are not successfully completed are the associated "attempts," which are separate and distinct violations. An attempt to commit a crime is an act done with specific intent to commit the particular crime, and proximately tending to but falling short of its consummation. There must be an apparent possibility to commit the crime in the manner specified. Thus, if a man attempts without extraneous aid to steal a two-ton statue by lifting it and carrying it away, there is no attempted crime because of the impossibility of successful consummation.

To be an attempted crime, there must be intent to commit the particular crime and an act or series of acts which would result in the crime's actual commission if there were no interruption by circumstances outside the doer's will. An intent to commit a crime not accompanied by an overt act to carry out the intent does not constitute an attempt. For example, a purchase of matches with intent to burn a house is not an attempt. If, however, a flame were set to the house in such a way as to eventually ignite the place, it would be an attempt, even if the rain or wind extinguished the flame before material damage to the premises resulted.

It is not an attempt if, when the act is completed, no crime results even if the accused intended to commit a crime. Thus, if a man shoots a bullet into a log, believing it to be his sleeping enemy, it is not attempted murder.

To render an act criminal, a wrongful intent must always be present. The criminal intent, however, may be presumed if the necessary or probable consequences of the act were wrongful or harmful, and if the act were deliberately committed. Drunkenness or being under the influence of drugs is not an excuse for a crime committed while in that condition; but it may be considered as affecting mental capacity to entertain a specific criminal intent where such intent is a necessary element of the offense. Imbecility, extreme youth or extreme age, idiocy, or any other condition indicating a mental abnormality may be considered for the purpose of determining whether the abnormality affected the mental capacity to entertain criminal intent in the specific crime.

Whenever it becomes important to prove guilty knowledge or intent in connection with the doing of a certain act, in order to preclude the possibility that the act was performed in good faith, it is proper to show that the accused has been guilty of similar offenses on prior occasions. Evidence of other crimes is also admissible in proving intent when it shows a common plan or scheme. Any act committed by the accused which rationally and reasonably interpreted would indicate a probable design is admissible to show intent. Thus, getting a revolver out of pawn a few days before a murder is admitted to show deliberate intent. Sharpening a knife just before an affray in which it is used is admitted to be an act of preparation.

Threats to do an act always create a probability that it may be done, and they are admissible against the accused to show his intent; if the person threatened is injured or killed, the threat furnishes ground to presume that he who threatened the act was the perpetrator or instigator.

The rules defining the crime of arson vary in many states, but most statutory rules break it down to three degrees which provide generally as follows: First-degree arson is committed when a person wilfully sets fire at night to a dwelling house in which there is a human being, or when he wilfully sets fire at night to a vehicle, vessel, or other structure, not a dwelling, which contains to his knowledge a human being. Second-degree arson is (a) an act of burning in the day time which if committed at night would have been first-degree arson; or (b) an act of wilfully setting fire to a dwelling house at night in which there is no human being; or (c) an act of wilfully setting fire to a vessel, car, vehicle, building, structure, or erection, which is at the time insured against loss or damage by fire, with intent to defraud the insurance company. Third-degree arson is committed by a person who wilfully sets fire to a vessel, vehicle, or any structure or erection under circumstances not amounting to arson in the first or second degrees. The subject of arson, especially as it applies to the insurance investigator, will be referred to in greater detail in a subsequent chapter.

Assaults generally are defined by statute as attacks upon another either with intent to kill, or while in the commission of a felony, or with intent to injure. The various degrees into which this crime is subdivided depend on whether or not a weapon, poison, or other object or substance was used by the attacker in consummating the assault, whether the intent was to injure or kill the victim, or whether the assault was committed incidentally to the commission of another crime.

Bigamy exists when a person who, having a husband or wife living, marries another if his prior marriage has not been dissolved by any judicial decree. Some jurisdictions hold that an absence for five successive years by one spouse from another, coupled with the belief that the missing spouse is dead, will act as a bar to a bigamy prosecution if a second marriage is contracted.

Burglary is also generally divided into three degrees in most states. The crime itself consists of the breaking into and entering a dwelling, building, room, or apartment of another with intent to commit some crime therein. The different degrees depend on factors such as whether the incident takes place at night or in the daytime; whether a human being is legally present on the burgled premises; whether the violator is armed; whether he has a confederate; or whether he assaults a person during the commission of the burglary.

Conspiracy is the crime which is subject to more statutory amplification in the various states than any other violation. It is the crime with which every investigator, both civil and criminal, will come into frequent contact.

The general rule defining conspiracy is that it is an unlawful agreement between two or more persons to carry out an unlawful act. The unlawful agreement is not sufficient to secure a conviction if there is no overt act. The overt act may be legal in itself, but it must be present. For example, two men meet in the back room of a saloon and plan the robbery of the local bank the following day. All details are agreed on, and the two men agree to meet at a designated point the next day. If they are arrested immediately, no actionable crime of conspiracy has yet been committed for lack of the overt act. If one of the conspirators lawfully purchased an automobile for the getaway, however, pursuant to their agreement, the crime of conspiracy is completed, by the overt act which was a lawful act in itself.

Great latitude is allowed in conspiracy cases in the admission of circumstantial evidence, because the jury is entitled to have in its possession every admissible fact which has a bearing on, or a tendency to prove, the points in issue. There must be a unity of design or purpose, and the common design is the essence of the conspiracy. The evidence that each of several persons acted illegally and with the same end in view will not establish a charge of conspiracy unless proof is adduced that such acts were done pursuant to a mutual agreement. If a person understanding the unlawful character of the transaction, and with a view to furthering the illegal enterprise or scheme encourages, advises, counsels, or in any manner assists in its performance, he becomes a conspirator. It is well to remember that any co-conspirator is a competent witness against his co-defendants.

Some jurisdictions contain statutes defining embezzlement in essence as the fraudulent appropriation of property by a person to whom it has been entrusted, or into whose hands it has lawfully come. The gist of the offense is a breach of trust, arising from a fiduciary relationship or an employer-employee relationship existing between the owner and the person converting the property. Its most common application is to the agent or employee who appropriates to his own use money or chattels received or held by him for his employer.

The crime of larceny is the unlawful carrying away or taking of things personal without right, and with intent to deprive the rightful owner of his property. Many states by statutory enactment, have made embezzlement a kind of larceny and consider larceny any act whereby a rightful owner is fraudulently or wrongfully deprived of his property. New York State's statute on larceny embraces taking the property from the owner wrongfully; obtaining it by the aid of false representations, either orally or in writing; converting property wrongfully to one's own use while it is in one's possession, custody, or control as a bailee, servant, attorney, agent, clerk, trustee, public officer, or employee. New York State also has a specific statute declaring that any person submitting a false written statement, financial or otherwise, for the purpose of procuring credit, shall be guilty of a violation.

The crime of fraud is the gain of an advantage to another's detriment by deceitful or unfair means. It may be actual, as where there is a deliberate misrepresentation, concealment, or fraudulent intent; or constructive, where the court infers it from the nature of the occurrence. Criminal frauds are generally defined by statute under the heading of the respective crimes when fraud is practiced in perpetrating the specific unlawful act.

The crime of forgery is an unauthorized alteration of a document, or a signature on a document, with intent to defraud. Alteration may include counterfeiting, erasure, obliteration, or mutilation. Some jurisdictions provide that the crime of uttering a forged instrument is a separate and distinct offense. For instance, if a person accepts a check knowing that the proper payee's name has been forged, and he then cashes this check at a bank by endorsing it with his own name, he has not actually forged the document, but he has uttered a forged instrument. The general definition is that a person who, knowing that a document is forged or altered, disposes of it or offers it with intent to defraud, is guilty of uttering a forged instrument.

Various degrees of forgery are prescribed by the statutes, depending largely on the type of document forged or altered. The document may consist of an instrument written or printed, or partly written and partly printed or engraved, and it may include tickets, checks, books of account, stocks and bonds, wills, letters, receipts, endorsements, public documents such as deeds or marriage, or certificates; in fact, any material document evidencing a fact is subject to forgery.

The crime of murder is a form of homicide. Murder is the unlawful killing of a human being. If the unjustified killing resulted from a deliberate premeditated design or was perpetrated while in the commission of a felony, it is murder in the first degree. The punishment for this crime is usually death, except in those states which prohibit capital punishment.

Most states consider the crime to be murder in the second degree when it is committed with a design to effect the death of the victim but without premeditation.

The crime of manslaughter is also a form of homicide. It exists when the accused kills someone without intending to effect death. There are various degrees of manslaughter, depending on whether the accused was committing a misdemeanor, committed the act in the heat of passion, aided the deceased to abort, was trespassing, or was culpably negligent. There are other incidents and situations defined by law as manslaughter, but the foregoing is a list of the most common elements involved in this crime.

The crime of perjury is a false statement under oath, wilfully made in regard to a material fact. The perjurious statement may be made in any document, affidavit, deposition, or certificate, or it may be made orally in court, at a hearing, proceeding or inquiry, or on any other occasion where testimony under oath is submitted. Wilfulness must be shown in perjury, and it does not exist when the testimony is given under an honest mistake, erroneous assumption, or misapprehension, and when the witness honestly believes the testimony given to be true. Even if falsity and wilfulness appear, the statement must be made with regard to a material fact.

For example, a person who, in the course of a heated discussion with friends, boasts that he once killed a lion and would be willing to sign an affidavit to that effect to substantiate his statement, is not committing perjury upon the execution of the affidavit, even if his statement is false. There is no materiality to his statement under the circumstances stated. Materiality is a question of fact depending upon the particular points in issue. In the current example, if the affiant lived in a community which paid a bounty to anyone who killed a lion, the submission of the false affidavit in order to collect the bounty would be perjury, because in this case the false statement is made with reference to a material fact.

The investigator should always be alert for perjury by his witness if the latter makes sudden changes in his story. It sometimes happens that an unscrupulous adversary has influenced the witness and his testimony. Whenever any person wilfully procures or induces another to commit perjury, he becomes guilty of the crime of subornation of perjury.

The crime of robbery is the unlawful taking of personal property from the person or the presence of another against his will by means of force, violence, or fear of injury. The various degrees of robbery depend on such factors as the possession of dangerous weapons, the use of an accomplice, the infliction of bodily injury, or the placing of the person robbed in fear of personal injury. There must be actual violence or intimidation employed against the owner of the property stolen, although the amount of violence used is immaterial if the robber overcomes the resistance of the person robbed or places him in such a position that he makes no resistance. It is equally robbery when the robber by threats or menace puts the victim in such fear that he is warranted in making no resistance.

The subpoena is the instrument whereby witnesses are compelled to attend a court or other tribunal, by virtue of the command contained in this writ. The *subpoena duces tecum* is personally served upon a person who has in his possession any book, instrument, etc., the production of which is desired, commanding him to bring with him the specified document for production at the trial.

Many fields of investigation require the investigator to continue his efforts in a given case after he submits his report of investigation. In these fields the investigator is charged with carrying the matter through the trial. He acts as a complete overseer of his case, holding together the framework of his investigation. He also functions as the guide and supply man for the attorney, who merely, in effect, uses the ammunition handed to him. This is one main reason why the investigator must have a speaking knowledge of the ingredients of the most prevalent major crimes, and of common court and trial procedures.

One of the legal pitfalls in which the investigator will often find himself is that he becomes involved in a mass of subject matter of an extremely technical nature. When the subject matter is such that the proper conclusion to be drawn from the facts depends on professional or scientific knowledge or skill, qualified experts may express their opinions about the proper inference to be drawn from a given set of facts as an aid to the jury in reaching its conclusion. The investigator should ascertain before trial what evidence merits expert testimony, and he should have this phase of the pre-trial preparation ready for the trial counsel.

Another pitfall which has ruined many a good investigator is the glare of publicity in which he may find himself when the trial commands public interest. While a well-publicized criminal case resulting in a conviction may act as a deterrent to others in committing similar offenses, especially in insurance fields, the investigator should be discreet and careful in his contact with reporters. His value in a community as an investigator is diminished when his picture is plastered all over the newspapers, and when he and his occupation become known to all newspaper readers in his community. He literally becomes a "marked man."

While the investigator should not surround himself with any air of mystery, or build around himself a romantic halo, if he is one of the central figures during a trial he must remember that remarks of his which would be seemingly casual and unimportant elsewhere take on sudden meaning and significance. Prudence dictates that the investigator, whether in court or out, keep his own counsel, indulge in no garrulity, and communicate his information only to those persons or officials properly entitled to receive it.

CHAPTER NINE

SCIENCE IN INVESTIGATION

SCIENTIFIC advances in the investigative field since the turn of the century have been phenomenal. These forward steps, the tempo of which was accelerated by techniques developed in World War II, are still progressing at a rapid pace.

Unfortunately, in numerous instances the scientific aids which should be a boon to the investigator turn out to be boomerangs, a paradoxical result attributable to the ignorance of the average investigator when confronted with a complex scientific problem. The mistake is made when the investigator, recognizing a salient feature necessitating scientific action, attempts to find the scientific solution himself. It is the same as if a well-read layman, correctly diagnosing a pain in his lower right quadrant as appendicitis, proceeded to operate on himself.

Scientific investigation is so intricate and ranges through so many different fields that it utilizes the best brains and the ablest specialists in dozens of unrelated professions. It is impossible for the investigator to master all of these complexities. He may be a specialist in an activity such as fingerprinting or ballistics, but it is sufficient if he can recognize a situation where indications point to the necessity of a specific scientific test. He should then procure the services of a person who is properly qualified by experience and background to perform such a test.

There are certain basic operations, however, which a well-versed investigator will perform himself. How far he should go without outside help depends on the circumstances in the case and the inherent knowledge he possesses of the subject matter. He must keep his mind continually alerted for all little things no matter how trifling, because it is the minor, unplanned details which become, with the aid of science, the downfall of violators.

The investigator should familiarize himself with the sources of scientific aid available in his community. In most jurisdictions State Police Headquarters possess scientific laboratories which are of inestimable service to the investigator. Technical aid may also be procured from police departments in large cities, county detectives' offices, sheriffs' offices, medical examiners, museums, university research laboratories, and government bureaus including the laboratories of the F.B.I. In addition, private chemists, physicians, trade specialists, artisans, handwriting experts, and so forth may be consulted. Many industries and many protective organizations, notably in the insurance field, maintain laboratories staffed by experts. Some large retail stores have their own research bureaus to test merchandise. Any one of these sources can well be adapted to an investigator's needs.

The purpose of this chapter is to acquaint the investigator with some of the latest and most commonly used scientific methods in investigation, and to enable him to recognize a situation where specific technical aids should be employed to force the solution.

It is hoped that civil investigators will use to a greater extent than heretofore those scientific aids which are sometimes regarded erroneously as an exclusive adjunct of criminal investigation.

QUESTIONED DOCUMENTS

In examining questionable documents, the foundation of the laboratory tests to be applied rests on a scientific comparison of the disputed handwriting with a standard which is conceded to be the handwriting of the person involved. It is the established evidence, introduced as a criterion, with which all the suspected writing must be compared.

The investigator should obtain conceded standards from such sources as indicate that the originator had no desire at such a time and place to disguise his handwriting. Such samples may often be obtained from letters, diaries, checkbooks, canceled checks, income-tax returns, leases, driver's licenses, applications for marriage licenses, car registrations, voting and public library registrations, and employment records. The scientific handwriting expert will find individual peculiarities in every word of the conceded standards, and he will then look for the recurrence of these characteristics in the disputed writings.

In a specific handwriting being examined there may be a similarity of several letters with the writing of other persons, but it is beyond the law of probability that any two persons could possess the same persistent and distinctive traits pertaining to every letter of the alphabet.

If a recorded document sought to be used as a standard is not available or is insufficient for the purposes of comparison, the person from whom such a standard is desired may be asked to write a letter or other text. In such cases, whatever is to be written should be dictated by the investigator. To facilitate the task for the handwriting expert, the investigator should provide the same type of paper if possible for the standard of comparison as was used in the disputed writing, for instance, postcards, letterheads, lined paper, or telegraph blanks. All of the words in the disputed handwriting should be used several times in the text dictated by the investigator. The dictation should proceed at a reasonably rapid rate to obviate any attempt on the part of the writer to disguise his handwriting. Particular care should be exercised in the repetition of words originally misspelled to learn if the same words are again misspelled. The same color of ink or the same kind of pencil should be used, and the writer should not be allowed to read back the text but should be kept writing steadily.

It is possible to determine by several well-known scientific tests the type of ink used, its age, and the country of origin. Instruments such as the photometer, the X-ray, ultraviolet ray, tintometer, microscope, camera, spectograph, and various chemicals are used by the expert in laboratory tests involving paper and ink.

The investigator should exercise particular care in noting all watermarks on the paper, because the age and source of the paper may be determined in many instances by this means. Care should be taken to examine the handwriting in the folds of documents. When a paper is folded, some fibers are broken, and the properties of absorption are altered. Most documents are written before they are folded, and if it appears by the fold that the ink line is spread and not even, this is an indication of additional writing after the completion of the original manuscript. Expert laboratory tests will show by disclosing the difference in ink or pens used whether additions were made.

Handwriting crimes are intellectual crimes, and the investigator must cope with the very cleverest criminal brains if he must match wits with forgers. The investigator must be one step ahead of the criminal, who in turn strives to lead the field.

It is a matter of common knowledge among skilful forgers that a clever investigator will subject paper to intensive investigation if the age of the document is a matter in issue. As a result, the practice is becoming increasingly prevalent for frauds and cheats to buy old books and Bibles and to cut the blank pages from the volumes. If the year of printing is stated in the book, it establishes the period, and if a fraudulent document is to be prepared allegedly dated from that period, this paper is used. The authentic paper from that period presents a definite obstacle in ascertaining the genuineness of the writing.

There have been an increasing number of frauds perpetrated in recent years because of the wrongful use of official certifications. The criminal in these cases will obtain certified copies of innocuous documents, such as condemnation proceedings or corporate charters. He will then steam off the seal of the court or the insert to which it is attached and affix it to the spurious document, later attempting to pass it off as a duly certified copy of a court record. Vigilance in scrutinizing and examining important documents for any irregularity in conventional form will pay dividends.

The entire financial empire which Ivar Kreuger built was based on government bonds which he had printed to the tune of twenty-five million dollars and to which he himself signed the purported names of the government officials. Not one bond was placed in circulation. They were merely put up as collateral for loans and were considered as genuine assets for many years. How many other such securities are resting as collateral in bank vaults, the imagination only may conceive. The example is cited to show the magnitude of operations possible in forgery.

The investigator may be called upon to ascertain the source of troublesome or "poison-pen" communications. The expert should always be enlisted in such instances. However, if the suspects can be narrowed down to a group operating in an office, the surreptitious placing of marked postage stamps in their desks may help to effect a solution. The stamps can be coded unobtrusively in such a way that the sender will be known. A method of marking generally used is the cutting out of a specified number of the tiny edges joining the perforations. This does not mutilate or deface the stamp, and the number of edgings form a foolproof means of identification.

Emphasis is laid on the fact that an accredited handwriting expert must be sought out as distinguished from a graphologist. Handwriting is a graphic extension of a personality and a visible record of established physical habits and emotional balance. Illness, discouragement, senility, and degeneration are reflected as changes in handwriting. Success and development of powers are similarly reflected. Like all sciences, graphology has its quacks. One well-known graphologist went so far as to state in a lengthy treatise that women who habitually write with large loops are persons of loose morals.

Unfortunately, in many communities some handwriting experts are associated with the practice of graphology, and the danger to an investigator's case can become very real if the expert he uses can be led, on cross-examination, into the dangerous, still theoretical field of character reading from handwriting.

The investigator should exercise extreme care in the handling of a disputed document. If it should be soiled, he should not attempt to cleanse or erase the document. It is good practice to take any valuable document which may be the subject of a dispute to a photographer to have an actual photograph made. This is especially true if the document is in the investigator's possession temporarily. By having the document photographed, the existence of a true reproduction is assured in case an unscrupulous person attempts to change the original subsequently. The important factor is also established that a disinterested person—the photographer—can be called upon to produce the original plate. It also assures the existence of a true copy in case the original document is lost or destroyed.

From the moment a questionable document comes into the possession and custody of the investigator, it should be carefully preserved in the condition in which it is found. Not only are the handwriting, typing, printing, and engraving important, but folds, perforations, or torn edges may furnish clues as to origin and genuineness. Any such document should be placed immediately in a cellophane holder large enough to hold it without folding. Thereafter the document should not be handled more than necessary and, if possible, it should be inspected and examined before the expert receives it without removing it from the transparent folder. It should not be allowed to become wet, torn, or crumpled, and it should be kept from excessive dampness, heat, or dryness.

TYPEWRITERS

Variations in typewritten documents can be detected as definitely as those in fingerprints or handwriting. In the early days of the typewriter it was used successfully as the ally of the forger. Pages of spurious matter were added to wills, and fraudulent additions were made to documents either marginally or by the insertion of additional pages. There was no difference of handwriting to invite attention, and for a while forgers enjoyed a Roman holiday. Today typewriting is an excellent means of following the wrongdoer, and it is the ally of the scientific investigator in his efforts to detect culprits.

Ever since the appearance of the Remington typewriting machine in 1871, surprisingly complete factory records have been kept by the manufacturers pertaining to styles and changes in type. Competent examiners of questioned documents have in their possession complete records of factory changes in machines, and often a glance at a questioned document will reveal to the practiced eye the model, the manufacturer, the year of manufacture, and the year when manufacture was discontinued.

The machines which tool the parts of typewriters vary with each operation, and each change is microscopically reflected in the machine. The machines develop other changes and peculiarities in the course of usage. The ribbons differ, as shown by microscopic examination of the number of threads. No piece of paper can be inserted into a machine the second time exactly like the first time; this makes it possible for laboratory tests to show if data was added to a document by re-insertion into a machine.

There are several points the investigator should always seek to have determined by an expert in the evaluation of a questionable typewritten document. It may be necessary to ascertain if the document was written on a particular typewriter, or whether the entire document was typed on one or more machines. It may be necessary to determine if extraneous data have been written at the close of a paragraph, at the top or bottom margins, in the form of interlineations, or whether entire sheets have been inserted. The time element may be important in ascertaining the approximate time of typing, whether the document was written at one time or over a period of time, and whether more than one machine was used during the various periods of typing.

In involved documents and wills, if there is suspicion that an additional sheet was inserted with the original, the investigator should not attempt to unstaple, unclip, or unfasten the mechanical devices holding the sheets together but should leave that to the expert. The sheets had to be unfastened in order to insert the spurious sheet. As a result, when the document was refastened, the new holes made will be unlike those made during the original stapling process and can be detected in a minute examination. Such evidence can be used in attacking the validity of the document.

Erasures and eradications are fairly easy to detect. By simply holding a document up to the light an erasure or abrasion can be noticed because the document is thinner in such a place. Eradication leaves chemical residuary matter on the paper, and this is easy to detect when subjected to a laboratory test.

FINGERPRINTS

The corrugations on the fingers of all human beings begin to form about three months before birth. From the instant of formation, through birth to death and for some time after death, they do not vary one iota in pattern. Certain occupations like wood finishing or masonry wear down the ridges to make the pattern less distinct, but a short period of time spent away from the work causing this abrasion will restore the natural pattern completely. For this reason, attempts at mutilation fail because furrows will form on the new skin or scar tissue in the same immutable pattern.

Of the hundreds of thousands of fingerprints sent annually to the Federal Bureau of Investigation for classification, about sixty-five percent have prior records.

No two fingerprint patterns have ever been found to be alike. There are cases on record where clever criminals, with the aid of unscrupulous engravers, had plates made of spurious fingerprints and impressed these plates on rubber gloves which were worn at the scene of a crime. However ingenious this method is, it has failed, and it is as yet not a factor to be reckoned with because of the inability of the engravers to duplicate the pores on the ridges. Poroscopy is the examination of sweat pores for identification; it has been discovered that these pores have different patterns for each finger and for each human being. The pattern does not change during life, and if the skin is injured, the fingerprint pattern will grow back in its original fashion.

Because of the common use of fingerprints for identification, the clever criminal today unfortunately uses gloves invariably at the scene of a crime. There is no question that this hampers the investigation, although steps have been made in identifying the wearer by the impression of the gloves, which leave their own indelible stamp of thread formation and weave. The nervousness of a violator results in a profuse exudation of sweat, which makes the glove greasy and prone to leave its impression. The investigator should pick up any suspicious gloves, not only for this purpose but for expert examination for particles of dust, glass, sawdust, dirt, or fibers, as these microscopic specks will often be associated with the scene of violation.

A thorough search should be made of the scene of the crime and the subject matter of the violation for latent fingerprints. These are prints which are at first generally invisible but may be revealed by the use of fine-grained powders. The oils and acids excreted through the sweat pores of the skin leave a distinct, colorless pattern when the skin comes into contact with an object.

Because of the general invisibility of the fingerprints, an iodine fume "gun" may be used to blow the fumes over the area where the suspected fingerprints are believed to be affixed. The fumes color the impression for a period of about ten minutes, so that it becomes visible to the naked eye. The impression may then be photographed or powdered. The fine powder grains brushed lightly on the impression will become attached to the excretion of the sweat pores, forming the pattern of the fingerprint. The raised fingerprint is then given a degree of permanence so that it will not dry up with the drying of the fluids or revert back to its colorless state with the wearing off of the iodine fumes. The investigator should carefully label the fingerprints taken as evidence and properly preserve them by placing them in receptacles which will prevent the prints from becoming obliterated.

Often a fingerprint may be affixed to an object which cannot be bodily transported, such as a safe or an automobile. If it is not feasible at the time to photograph the fingerprint, it may be "lifted" by placing cellulose foil, a material similar to Scotch tape, gently over the raised print. Uniform pressure applied will cause the powders on the fingerprint to adhere to the sticky surface of the tape. Extreme care should be used in this operation, because the basic pattern of the latent print is generally destroyed during the process of lifting. When this operation is successfully accomplished, the foil contains the print, and it may be preserved for evidence or future investigation.

While it is much easier to find latent prints on a glossy surface, they have been found and successfully developed on objects made of wood, paper, leather, and cloth. They have not as yet been found on human skin. The progress of developing latent fingerprints on paper has been rapid in recent years, and unless a letter has been handled and re-handled dozens of times, the impressions left by the sender can usually be ascertained. The technique of lifting latent fingerprints is fairly simple and can be mastered to a great degree of proficiency by the average investigator without undue effort. Several types of kits for lifting latent fingerprints, containing all of the essential requisites, are on the market.

The importance of a case may sometimes warrant that the evidence be subjected to every conceivable care, because of the need for more competent authority to conduct the search for fingrprints. In such cases furniture may be dismantled and the suspected parts taken to a laboratory; glass panes may be cut out, and parts of automobiles may be removed to a laboratory. Extreme care should be used in packing the objects to avoid friction of any sort.

The investigator should use extreme care not to disturb, brush against, obliterate, move, or trample those areas or articles where fingerprints are likely to be found. For instance, in handling a "poison-pen" letter, the document should be placed in an envelope and touched only by holding the extreme edges. Some investigators use pliers in handling such documents. Similarly, in automobile theft cases or crimes when an automobile was used, extreme care should be exercised in examining the rear view mirror. This object is a lush hunting ground for the investigator, because the violator in most cases readjusts the mirror in his desire for better vision, prompted by the fear of pursuit.

The use of the camera when possible is strongly advocated for the taking of photographs of (a) latent fingerprints; (b) visible fingerprints, such as those left by blood or dirt impressions; and (c) fingerprints found on plastic surfaces such as putty or wax. The secondary measures for perpetuating the prints are to be used only incidentally to the camera as its aid in giving the fingerprints a degree of permanency.

It frequently becomes necessary for the investigator in both civil and criminal matters to obtain the fingerprints of a suspect without his knowledge in order that a further check of his background may be made by this means. If the suspect can be interviewed, he may be shown a photograph to see if he recognizes the subject. The photograph should be in a glass or plastic frame, and it should be sandwiched between two pieces of glass. The object should be handed to the suspect. If the investigator deliberately drops a highly polished cigaret case while carrying on a conversation with the suspect, the latter may pick it up first. If the suspect smokes, a highly polished plastic or metal lighter may be passed to him for lighting his cigaret.

If no such close contact with the suspect can be established discreetly, he may be tailed to a restaurant or saloon. His empty whiskey glass or a drinking glass he used at the table where he had his meal may sometimes be filched. The difficulty in these instances is that the waiter or bartender may also leave his fingerprints on the object. It is sometimes possible to enlist the aid of the bartender or waiter, who will place a clean, polished glass before the suspect and remove it immediately after he has had a drink from the container. Sometimes the help of a mailman may be enlisted. A registered or special-delivery letter may be sent to the suspect, and the mailman will be asked to have the receipt for the mail signed by the suspect with a wide-barreled fountain pen which has been filled, cleaned, and polished for the purpose.

THE LIE DETECTOR

The lie detector is still regarded with a jaundiced eye by the old-type roundsman who considers his hairy fists and blackjack the best lie detector. In spite of this, although the instrument is still in its adolescent stage, it has proved itself efficient in so many instances that its use is general in all parts of the United States.

The instrument is based on the emotional reaction of the subject, and its success lies not only in its aid in determining guilt, but as a distinct aid in eliminating the innocent as suspects.

The two types of instrument which are most widely used are the cardio-pneumo type or polygraph, which records pulse, blood pressure, and respiration, and the psychogalvanometer or pathometer, which records the reaction of the sweat glands of the hands. Both types are based on the reaction of the subject to his secret thoughts when he hears something which is related to the crime.

Most large enforcement units have working arrangements with hospitals, universities, or scientific laboratories for the use of the lie detector under the supervision of an expert.

PHOTOGRAPHY

Recording the human face for identification is by no means the only service performed by the camera in the field of investigation. When the trial of any issue takes place, a word picture is sought to be portrayed to the court of incidents, occurrences, or events which are in dispute. What better way is there to supplement this picture than by actual facsimiles of the events, rather than the verbal descriptions dependent on memory or motive? It also goes without saying that a photograph impresses a jury by its accuracy and force, and it is a continuing reminder of the events it seeks to explain when taken into the jury room for study and consideration.

During the past years the motion-picture camera has come into wide use and strangely enough, more in civil than in criminal investigation. The miniature camera is easily obtainable, and is in wide use. The vest-pocket watch camera was described previously. Actually, any small camera can be adapted for use in a flashlight or fountain pen. One of the cleverest innovations for the placing of a camera was developed by an insurance adjuster, who has a complete camera assembled in one of the headlights in his automobile, controllable from the dashboard.

The average investigator can easily learn the technique of simple photography, whether it is with an ordinary camera, hidden camera, miniature camera, or movie machine. If any technical difficulties are anticipated, however, such as lighting problems, angle photography, the necessity for the use of the telephoto lens, complicated fingerprints, or interior photography, an attempt should be made to employ an expert photographer.

Photomicrography is the science of combining the microscope and the camera in search of clues not apparent to the naked eye. It is used widely in the examination of hairs, fibers, dust particles, perforations on paper, and other minute objects. Its use is becoming very prevalent in the insurance field in the photographing of precious gems. Every precious stone is different when seen under the photomicroscope, and every flaw becomes a landmark toward eventual recovery of the gem if stolen.

The fluoroscope camera enables the instrument to pierce solid matter and to photograph objects not visible to the naked eye. It is an adaptation of the fluoroscope used in medical science, and its chief use in investigation is to probe the interior of suspicious packages suspected of containing bombs or other infernal devices. It may, however, be used by an investigator whenever he is confronted with any situation where such a device might be of assistance.

Radiography is frequently used in attempts to read the contents of sealed letters. If the missive is closely written and folded, it is sometimes difficult to evaluate the contents fully. As a matter of fact, the reading of sealed mail by the use of the X-ray was believed to be so prevalent that lead-lined envelopes, which stop the penetration of these rays, have been placed on the market.

It is of paramount importance that the camera be used widely in the insurance fields of liability, property damage, accident, health, and workmens' compensation. The ability of a man to perform hard physical work, when he contends that he is sick or disabled, can be proved by the photograph in addition to discreet tailing. After an accident, the sooner a photograph is taken of the scene of the accident, the sooner these facts become fixed and stated, not subject to possible warping and misconstruction at the time of the trial when the memories of witnesses become dim, not only because of the passage of time, but sometimes through design.

The ultraviolet light has become an important factor in photography. It is produced by a lamp made of quartz which allows an uninterrupted flow of ultraviolet rays. Many objects, when subjected to ultraviolet rays, notably questioned documents, show the contrasts effected by erasures, alterations, and mutilations.

Frequently situations may arise where it is impracticable or impossible to photograph scenes or objects. In lieu thereof, sketches may be made as evidence of an accurate, objective description before anything in the scene described was altered, moved, or destroyed. Consistency should be used in the measurements, and if pacing is employed, the name and approximate pace length of the pacer should be stated. The sketch should contain the compass directions and should be drawn to scale. The person making the drawing should take his own measurements and should not rely on another person, as difficulty might be encountered in introducing the sketch in evidence.

MICROSCOPY

The science of microscopy is the bulwark of science in investigation. Anyone may look through a microscope, but only an expert can understand the meaning of what is seen. It is almost impossible to commit a violation without leaving some physical trace, however minute. A trace may be a fingernail clipping, a hair, a piece of string, a button, a drop of blood, a speck of dandruff, dust from a shoe, thread from clothing, or a hint of a toolmark.

The results obtained from tiny bits of information are magical. The late Dr. Albert Schneider, Dean of the Berkeley, California, School for Police Officers, was a wizard at the microscope. At one time the police in a California town brought to him several sticks of dynamite, capped and fused, which had been found near the residence of a prominent citizen. Dr. Schneider carefully removed the paper wrappings in which the dynamite was enclosed. A small piece of string bound the dynamite sticks together. He subjected the string to several chemical tests and advised the incredulous police that the twine came from a farm on which would be found a stream of water, pine trees, black and white rabbits, a bay horse, a light cream-colored cow, and Rhode Island Red chickens. Investigation showed that the dynamite had been sold to a farmer whose farm tallied exactly with the place described by Dr. Schneider.

The dirt under a suspect's fingernails may be analyzed to

determine if it coincides with the locality of a violation. Dust in the clothes of a suspect or dirt on his shoes, may reveal the tale of the wearer's misdeeds. Tools will leave markings on materials softer than the tool itself. A cut telephone wire will carry markings of the cutter, and a burglary tool will impress distinctive markings on wood. Not only are the innumerable ridges and irregularities of the tool impressed upon its object, similar to the groovings of a gun barrel on a bullet, but microscopic particles cling to objects which are in forcible contact with each other.

Microscopic examination of hair will reveal whether it is animal or human; from what part of the body it came; whether it came from a man or a woman; how long it had been cut; and the age of its former possessor. If sufficient samples are available it may be determined that hair came from a particular individual after comparison with the conceded standards of the suspect. The characteristic dust of a person's profession is often attached to the hair.

Stains appearing to be blood can be tested by laboratory and microscopic examination to determine if they are in fact blood, and if so, whether it is animal or human blood.

The ear wax may be examined for the dust of a particular locality to fix the suspect's presence at that place. Sometimes microscopic examination of tobacco ashes will disclose the type of cigaret or cigar from which they came.

The investigator should become well versed in the assistance to be obtained from the use of the microscope in all fields of investigation.

THE SPECTROGRAPH

This instrument is of invaluable aid in identifying materials such as filings from a lock, or paint scraped from an automobile, as a part of a known sample. Any element has a unique or individualized spectrum or combination of lines peculiar to the particular element. Scrapings or tracings from the known object may be tested to see if fragments found elsewhere have been part of it. The spectrograph, the spectrogram, and the spectroscope are comparative newcomers to the field of investigation, but the merit of their use is proved, and they are no longer in the experimental or theoretical stages. The spectrograph and its variations have proved the presence of a violator at the scene of a crime innumerable times, and are now standard equipment with progressive law-enforcement agencies.

CHEMICAL ANALYSIS

Chemistry and physics have been the servants of the investigator for many years. Chemical analysis is a technical and specialized field and the investigator must be careful to have his exhibits intact and well identified for the expert. It is through the medium of chemistry that the characteristics of poisons, blood stains, dust, metals, and other substances are determined. No modern law-enforcement agency is without its own chemical laboratory today.

MOULAGE

Moulage means the fabrication of impressions of material or objects so transitory and temporary in nature that they would evaporate, melt, decompose, or otherwise be dispersed unless preserved by the fixity of plaster. Footprints, tire marks, wounds, teeth or bite marks, death masks, and tool markings are some of the evidentiary factors preserved by the use of moulage.

A walking picture of a man can be obtained from his footprints. Depth of print, length between steps, indentation of toe or heel, and angle of footsteps may give a comprehensive picture of weight, height, and peculiarities of walk. Individualities of shoes, reflected by sole or heel designs, nails, heel irons, toe protectors, and characteristics developed after wearing become as valuable as fingerprints in searching out the wearer. The application of plaster of Paris to footprints is a fairly simple technique, although in emergencies, imaginative investigators have used sulphur, tallow, lard, and even mixtures of flour and water with success. A thin coat of shellac is sprayed over the footprint, either with a spray gun or an atomizer, and allowed to harden before the plaster is applied.

In modern times, because of the importance of the motor car in everyday lives, tire-mark identifications have taken on increasing importance. The direction of the car may sometimes be determined by the heaps of dust stirred up. The length of the wheelbase as shown by the space between tire markings and the depth of the markings, which may indicate the weight of the car, often reveal the type of the vehicle. The automobile traveling in a straight line will leave the tracings of its rear tires only.

Once a tire marking is perpetuated by a cast, it will act as a major clue in locating the vehicle. It is one of the paradoxes of modern investigation that the comparatively simple task of indexing all known tire markings has been generally neglected. Tire marks, when considered in conjunction with other evidence of an automobile hit-run accident, such as pieces of broken lenses or other broken parts, may present a composite picture of the exact car which is the subject of the search.

Similar in procedure but different in principle is the practice of immersing the hand of a murder suspect or apparent suicide in melted paraffin until a thick coating of this substance is obtained. After the paraffin sets, it is gently removed from the hand, and the mold is examined for the presence of nitrates. These nitrates would be present on the inner surface of the mold if the modeled hand had recently fired a pistol, blown into the skin by the gases ejected from the backfire of the weapon.

This technique is extremely valuable to the insurance investigator probing a case where murder is indicated but where suicide is suspected, often because of the double- or triple-indemnity payments provided for in non-suicidal violent deaths. If the nitrate particles were found in a mold taken from the hands of the deceased, they would strongly indicate that the dead person had fired the lethal weapon himself.

The converse is also true when a murderer arranges the scene of a crime to make it appear like suicide by gunfire. The paraffin mold from the suspect's hands would show if he had fired the weapon.

THE MINE DETECTOR

The magnetic mine detector widely used in World War II is now generally regarded as a peacetime accessory of the investigator. Its uses are manifold, but its main usefulness is in locating hidden weapons such as guns and knives and in seeking out hidden loot of a metallic nature or that contained in a metallic receptacle.

THE SNOOPERSCOPE

This instrument, known during World War II as the sniperscope, is described in chapter VI.

PORTABLE X-RAY MACHINE

The portable X-ray machine, which can be transported to the scene of an investigation, may be used to examine the contents of packages, or it may be used in locating hidden objects in cases where the use of the mine-detector device is not practicable.

MICRO-ANALYTICAL BALANCE

This is one of the most delicate measuring instruments known to science. It can measure the minutest particle of material, and it is sensitive to one three-millionth of an ounce.

COLORIMETER

This machine indicates the difference in color between two solutions or transparent solids. By means of the electric photometer, commonly known as the electric colorimeter, analysis can be made accurately and quickly of blood, urine, ink, and other solutions.

BLOOD GAS APPARATUS

This contrivance is used to conduct examinations involving biochemistry, particularly that phase involving blood analysis. It is used to determine the presence of carbon dioxide in blood or plasma, as a measure of alkaline reserve, and of the oxygen capacity of the blood, and to detect carbon monoxide as evidence of poisoning.

SPOT-TEST OUTFIT

This equipment is used to identify unknown compounds. It is used in the production of spot colorations on absorbent paper or porcelain tiles; the formation of microcrystals which can be observed under a microscope; the development of colors in solution; and the precipitation of insoluble compounds which can be identified or weighed.

OXYGEN BOMB CALORIMETER

This machine measures heat in substances. By knowing the absolute heating effect, the chemist is aided in identifying many organic substances. It is used to analyze food, coal, oil, gas, and so forth.

Ph MACHINE

This machine is used to determine the alkalinity or acidity of a substance—the first step in most analytical procedures.

VISCOSIMETER

This device measures the ability of a substance to resist flow. When the viscosity of a given substance is known, the machine determines the nature of the substance from the viscosity factor. It is used to test paints, varnish, glass, flour, gelatin, ice cream, glue, starches, asphalt, chocolate, oils, dairy products, sugar and syrup solutions and dyes.

BAFFLE FURNACE

This device is a multiple-unit electric furnace used for drying precipitates, ash determinations, fusions, ignitions, and heating metals and alloys.

ELECTRO ANALYZER

This machine can rapidly detect the presence of metallic elements in solution. It can quickly determine the presence of gold, silver, platinum, zinc, lead, nickel, copper, tin, antimony, and mercury. It will also analyze brass, bronze, amalgams, and other similar alloys in solution.

THE DECELEROMETER

Skid marks show the approximate speed at which a car has been traveling before an accident. Brake tables analyze these marks, taking into consideration whether the vehicle had two-wheel or four-wheel brakes, or whether the road was wet or dry. These tabulations are not as exact, however, as is desired because road conditions such as rising or falling grades may affect the value of the calculations. The correctness of the formula upon which the tables are based is also disputable in view of the fact that varying braking conditions are found on different types of roads such as macadam, asphalt, concrete, dirt, washboard, brick, plank, or block highways.

The decelerometer will show the actual distance which the car in question will travel before stopping, scientifically and without guesswork, under the same conditions prevailing at the time of the accident.

OBLITERATED SERIAL NUMBERS

Serial numbers on guns, automobiles, machines, or other metal objects, which have been filed off or otherwise obliterated, can be read by employing a technical metallurgical process involving acid-inspired etchings. When the original numbers were impressed into the metal, the molecular structure of the metal directly underneath the area of the pressure underwent changes which can be brought out.

WOOD ANALYSIS

This embryonic science attained full maturity in the Lindbergh kidnapping case, when the kidnap ladder was traced to the defendant, Hauptmann, and his attic. The identification and association of wood objects can be made by the pitch streaks, annular rings, nail holes, grain characteristics, plane marks, cuttings, and knottings. It is even possible to identify sawdust as coming from a particular piece of wood.

INDELIBLE LAUNDRY MARKS

The invisible identifying mark of the laundry has become a matter of general practice in the trade. It is not visible to the naked eye, and it can be seen only when exposed to the ultraviolet ray. The mark is a symbol which identifies it with a particular laundry. Underwear, shirts, napkins, handkerchiefs, and bath towels should receive the investigator's attention when necessary. Several law-enforcement agencies have cataloged and filed thousands of laundry marks and associated them with the issuing laundries.

BALLISTICS

The development of forensic ballistics has resulted in a science that is unchallenged in its importance in the field of homicide criminology. In making a gun, the first step is to bore a hole through a cylindrical steel bar as the basis for the barrel. All modern small arms and rifles have rifled bores. These spiraled grooves inside the gun barrel spin the bullets, which are conical-shaped and adapted to the rifling. This process gives the missiles greater speed, power, and range. The grooves are made by a tool cutter which leaves its own identifying marks in the barrel, different with each gun because of the minute changes resulting to the tool in each operation. When the steel shavings, which result from the cutting edge of the tool, are dragged out of the barrel, a still more individualized pattern is etched on the inner surface of each gun barrel.

Every bullet fired from a particular gun carries the impressions of the peculiarities of the specific barrel. A conceded standard or comparison bullet must be obtained from a weapon for comparison with the bullet suspected of coming from the same gun. The microscopic markings on both bullets should be identical if they are fired from the same pistol.

The markings of the firing pins also have individual characteristics that warrant comparison for similarity. This is of special importance in those cases where the gun used is an automatic pistol. When this type of weapon is used the expended shells are automatically ejected and can usually be found at the scene of the shooting. If a revolver or other non-automatic gun is used, the criminal generally does not stop to eject the expended shell at the scene of the shooting, and as a result this item of important evidence is usually lacking.

Other less apparent marks can sometimes be detected when made by the extractor, ejector, or breechlock. A fairly comprehensive manufacturers' history of American small arms, specifications, changes, and characteristics is available. These tabulations give caliber, designs and styles, and explanation of the twist and groove dimensions of each model. The number and width of grooves and direction of twist for each type of gun are described. These tables are of invaluable aid to the investigator who is seeking to determine the make and type of an unknown firearm from the bullet in his possession. Powder marks on a victim may also help in ascertaining the distance and direction from which the shot was fired.

THE HELIXOMETER

This instrument is a take-off on the cystoscope and bronchoscope of medical science. It enables the ballistic expert to subject the interior of a gun barrel to the most searching scrutiny. It notes and measures the barrel's rifling, rust, and powder residue.

The proper preservation of exhibits for the action of the expert is of paramount importance. Articles containing stains should be wrapped in clean paper or placed in a clean container, labeled and identified, and deposited at the laboratory immediately for chemical analysis. Time may be of paramount importance, as physical properties of some stains change with the passage of time. If the stains are on a solid object, such as a floor or wall, the object containing the stains should be scraped and the scrapings should be brought to the expert.

Hair and fibers should be handled with tweezers preferably, and they should not be allowed to mix or come in contact with other similar substances. The exhibits should be placed in a clean white envelope which should be properly labelled. Dust and soil should not be placed in an envelope because of potential loss through the seams. A clean, glass container should be used for the purpose. Whenever a sample may consist of a fermenting liquid such as mash from an illegal distiller, care should be exercised not to seal or cork the sample, because the continued fermentation may cause the container to explode because of the formation of gases which seek an outlet. If it is advisable to seal such a sample, a bichloride of mercury tablet may be placed in the liquid. This will stop fermentation yet not destroy the efficacy of the sample for purposes of analysis. All samples which are poisonous should be so labeled.

The increasing number of hit-and-run drivers in recent years has made the laboratory analysis of paints a matter of special importance. The particles of paint that can be found at the scene of the accident, either on the body of the victim or on any other object in the vicinity, should be flaked off with a clean instrument and placed in a clean pill box. After a suspect is apprehended, a specimen of paint from his car may be compared with the particles found at the scene of the accident. The laboratory tests will show if both samples are identical.

It cannot be too strongly emphasized what great care must be used when preserving samples and exhibits for laboratory tests. Not only must the specimen be kept intact and without change in its original form, but complete data should appear to show where the sample was obtained, stating date and place, and what it purports to be. The signature or initials of the investigator taking the specimen should always appear on the identifying label.

CHAPTER TEN

CREDIT AND COLLECTION

CREDIT is the power to obtain money, goods, or services by giving a promise to pay money or goods on demand or at a specified date in the future. The entire system of credit is based on man's confidence in man. When it is realized that approximately 80 per cent of the nation's business is transacted on credit, the magnitude of this design in our economic pattern becomes very apparent. Some of the common documents used in our everyday lives evidencing credit transactions are meal checks, notes, bank checks, money orders, bonds, drafts, letters of credit, traveler's checks, railroad tickets, theater tickets, invoices, bills of any sort, insurance policies, pension or retirement contracts, war bonds, and a host of others.

The importance of properly obtaining competent credit information and the necessity of continually coping with the abuses arising in this complex activity create an important role for the investigator. The information received as a result of the investigation becomes the basis for action. The investigator in the credit field is the safety factor charged with policing his organization against losses resulting from bad credit risks. Inasmuch as the major portion of the average firm's business is transacted on credit, the responsibility of keeping losses down to a minimum is very great. The credit investigator must see to it that accounts which lead to losses are not opened, and he must rule on extensions of credit. If he is charged with making collections, his is the responsibility of getting the customers to make prompt payments, and to salvage the salvageable from "dead beats."

The basis for a good account is the care exercised in procuring information when the new account is opened. Sufficient information should be obtained by the investigator to justify a careful and thorough analysis. Detailed and careful investigation before credit is granted not only is the best insurance for prompt payment, but is the best assurance for eventual collection of the account.

Various sources of information should be continually used. Mercantile agencies, other creditors, trade-group meetings, credit bureaus, interchange organizations, attorneys, banks, financial publications, and credit manuals are but a few of the sources available. Nevertheless, somewhere along the chain of available prepared information, an investigator, many investigators in fact, conducted original investigations to obtain the data. The reports may be disseminated throughout the length and breadth of the land, but the work of investigators is behind them all.

In many cases a creditor will not be satisfied with existing information because of the lapse of time since the last report, or because of other important factors. He will then want a current, individualized investigation.

The suggestions contained in this chapter are primarily for the investigator who initiates the investigation and who creates the portfolio of information which is used as needed.

The controlling factor in granting credit is confidence in the debtor. The confidence in the debtor should be based on a blend of character and capital. While there is a difference of opinion which is the more important, the late J. P. Morgan defined character as a fundamental of banking and placed it in a position of greater importance than money. The applicant for credit should have those qualities of character which show him to be willing to meet his obligations. The credit investigator should seek out all available information on this point. The applicant's past history, criminal record if any, reputation in the neighborhood in which he lives, associates, clubs, and interests all may shed light on the subject.

Specific but discreet inquiry should be made about the applicant's mode of living, tendency to drink alcoholic beverages and to gamble to excess, proclivities for associating with women in extramarital affairs, truthfulness, age, experience, maturity in business, ability to be an executive, general education, success in prior and current enterprises, contributions to charities, activity in civic affairs, indications of narrowness or bigotry, and social ambitions, especially if there are manifestations of "keeping up with the Joneses." If the foregoing information is obtained, it will present a composite view of any individual who is the subject of a character analysis. In credit, of course, as in any other field of investigation, the amount of effort expended in the investigation depends on the importance of the transaction.

Specific attention should be directed toward the applicant's financial condition as represented by the data submitted by him in support of his allegation. Special scrutiny should be made of insurance carried, method of paying debts in the past, and the reliability of the auditors or agents who prepared the financial data for the applicant.

It is emphasized again that a little extra time spent in investigation *before* the credit commitment is made will expedite a future investigation in the event the risk is faulty. Merely closing the barn door is not sufficient. To insure recovery of the stolen horse, a bag of flour must be tied to his tail in order that a clear, unequivocal trail is plainly left to mark the way for his ultimate return.

In the basic questions to be asked of the applicant, a wide range of interrogations can be used, either in the form of a questionnaire or in an interview. In certain instances, not all of these questions need be asked, but the following master list is submitted to serve as a guide:

1. Full name of the applicant (with exact spelling and without the use of initials).
2. Date of birth.
3. Address and telephone number of the applicant.
4. Is residence an apartment or private dwelling?
5. Ownership of residence. Does applicant or any member of family own?
6. If applicant rents property, is there a lease? Who signed lease?
7. Address of landlord.
8. How is rent paid (check or cash)?
9. The name of the applicant's bank.
10. Is applicant married? If so, name of husband or wife.
11. Does applicant have children? If so what schools do they attend? Where are they employed, if they work?
12. Occupation of applicant.
13. Name and address of employer.
14. If private business, name and address of business.
15. Social security number.
16. If employed, length of employment on current job.
17. Previous places of employment.
18. Where was income tax return filed?
19. Is applicant an officer or director in any firm or corporation?
20. Does applicant have power of attorney from anyone or has he given such power to anyone?
21. Does applicant have a safety deposit box?
22. Does applicant have right of access to another's safety deposit box?
23. Does applicant have accident, health, or life insurance? If so, list policies.
24. Is applicant receiving benefits from any insurance policy such as accident or health?
25. Does applicant carry insurance on household goods? If so, how much?
26. Does applicant own real estate? If so, where?
27. Does applicant own an automobile?

28. Does applicant have a driver's license?
29. Does applicant's wife (or husband) own car *if he does not?*
30. Are there unsatisfied judgments against the applicant?
31. Does the applicant own any mortgages? Jewels? Notes?
32. Has applicant been sued at any time? If yes, when, where and by whom?
33. Has applicant applied for a loan from any bank or loan company in past five years? If yes, list details.
34. Has applicant issued any financial statement in the past five years? If yes, when and to whom?
35. Has applicant interest in the estate of any deceased person?
36. Has applicant made a will?
37. Is applicant or spouse recipient of benefits of any trust?
38. Has applicant ever been in bankruptcy?
39. Has applicant filed any certificates of doing business under a trade name?
40. Does anyone owe applicant money?
41. Was applicant ever convicted of any crime excluding ordinary traffic violations?
42. Complete list of clubs and organizations to which applicant belongs.
43. Complete list of schools and colleges attended by applicant.
44. Names of applicant's parents. If living, their address.
45. Names and addresses of brothers and sisters.
46. References.

It can readily be seen that the foregoing information will be helpful not only in a current analysis, but will prove to be of inestimable aid in effecting collection at a subsequent date in the event the debtor becomes non-co-operative.

Detailed questions need not be asked in all cases. A credit investigator develops a "feel" in many instances of the applicant's veracity. While it is advocated that detailed information be obtained in advance of a credit commitment, the question nevertheless arises, "How does the credit investigator know that the information submitted to him during the course of an interview is true?"

Many investigating firms have on file lists of outstanding places of interest in the large cities in the country. When a questionable applicant is interviewed about his prior residences, it can sometimes be ascertained if he is lying by casually asking him about a certain hotel, street, movie theater, park, or other place in a city listed as a prior residence. Some investigators knowing, for instance, the names of every movie theater in a designated city, will refer to a fictitious and nonexistent theater to see if the applicant will fall for the ruse and state that he is familiar with it. The application for marriage license, if the applicant is married, can supply a wealth of information for the test of veracity.

It has been proved thousands of times that the principal reason a defaulting debtor could not be found was because of the paucity of information received during the basic interview. The credit investigator is at an advantage in that the applicant seeks something and at that time will submit all data required in order to attain his needs. There are, of course, transactions which by their very nature will make many questions personally offensive to the applicant who is a potential customer. The investigator should employ a combination of tact and diplomacy in obtaining as much of the required information as possible without, at the same time, reaching the danger point where his firm might lose a customer. In the majority of cases the intentions of the applicant for credit are honest at the time it is requested, and the time is then ripe to procure all available information. Circumstances may force the applicant to equivocate later, and the information at that time might be evasive and questionable. The data received at the beginning of the relationship is most frequently the means whereby ultimate payment is effected.

The applicant for credit should be questioned in private to

avoid unnecessary embarrassment. If a form or questionnaire is used, it is sometimes wise to have the applicant fill out his own paper. Such procedure tends to gain the confidence of the person interviewed. During the course of checking the form, the investigator may intersperse a few additional pertinent questions. The questioning should be conducted in a steady, even tenor, without any breaks. In this way the subject will not have too much chance to think between questions and any uneasiness, hesitancy, or sign of emotion may indicate a misstatement.

The names of references should be requested. It is generally understood today that this source of information is not too dependable because the reference is usually a friend of the applicant. Nevertheless, the character of the applicant and the strata of society in which he moves is frequently indicated by those with whom he associates. In evaluating a reference, his occupation, office, or profession must be considered. A person holding public office as the result of political activity will be freer and easier with his authentication of the character of acquaintances than the clergyman, doctor, and other professional persons whose professions are bound to a rigorous code of ethics. If a reference is consulted, he should be asked the names of others with whom the applicant associates. These persons whom the applicant did not list may submit information in a more disinterested vein. In ascertaining the background of a credit applicant, the tradesmen who serve him such as the butcher, baker, milkman, newsboy, and his janitor will supply a comprehensive picture of his trustworthiness.

The credit investigator should know the community in which he operates, and when an address is given which indicates a lodging-house area, the matter should be one of special scrutiny. Similarly, when an applicant falls into certain occupational categories, indicating that he is a floater or itinerant worker, special care should likewise be taken in the investigation.

It is always good policy for the investigator to consult the applicant's employer by mail before credit is granted. Very frequently frauds and cheats will assume the name of another actual person. They may take the name and number of a taxi driver from the taxicab, and the name of the employer. Trolley cars and buses often have the names of their operators posted in the vehicle. The employer of an applicant should always be consulted, and the address of the applicant should be submitted to the employer for verification. In addition the age, personal description, marital status, social security number, length of time of employment, and other pertinent data should be submitted to the employer. If the applicant is a cheat, the information he supplies at the basic interview will not coincide with the information on file in the employer's office about the person whose name is to be assumed. This is practically a foolproof check to put a quietus on such frauds, and its only cost is that of a postage stamp.

Some firms are reluctant to take the time to answer lengthy inquiries, and it is therefore advisable to send the applicant's employer a questionnaire listing the information desired. Spaces should be provided for the answers to be submitted by the employer. A stamped, self-addressed envelope for the return of the questionnaire definitely expedites the reply.

Usually the most simple way of obtaining a lead to the whereabouts of a defaulting debtor is through his relatives, and if the applicant is married, the names of his wife's parents should always be obtained. There is an old adage:

A son is a son until he takes to him a wife;
A daughter is a daughter all the days of her life.

No matter where the defaulter moves, his wife will usually keep in touch with her parents.

The credit investigator who acts as agent of a financial house in gathering in the field and reporting the credit and standing of a credit risk is confronted with problems that are different from those of the investigator representing the firm granting credit directly to the applicant. The subject's place of business is visited; his stock and place of business are examined; its location and other factors are noted; and he is interviewed. Local sources of information are visited and every effort is made to verify and amplify the statements of the subject.

A financial statement is obtained from the risk, and his history of prior payment is checked with creditors with whom he has had dealings. The courthouse, bank, and register's office can be potential sources of information to round out a picture of the subject. A good source of information not too generally employed is the local newspaper office. If the risk was ever in print, the newspaper will have a file for him in which will be found all newspaper stories mentioning him. Every article or item concerning him should be read.

Judgments, corporate records, transfers of realty, trade-name certificates, mortgages, chattel mortgages, liens, prior suits, pending suits, and changes of name can be found in the county clerk's office or the county courthouse. The clerk of the United States District Court should not be overlooked for federal litigation or bankruptcy. Sometimes it may be advisable to obtain a history of a naturalization proceeding or a passport application. The federal court clerk will have jurisdiction of these records. The United States marshal should be consulted, if such a course is indicated, to determine if there are any libel proceedings pending. Local municipal offices will disclose building or fire violations.

The various city, state, and federal departments which are charged with granting licenses may be investigated if the matter is germane to the risk in question. In New York City, over seven hundred different kinds of work require licenses. They range from the sidewalk bootblack's license to a midwife's license.

In the field of credit investigation, license information becomes extremely valuable in certain instances, such as when the risk is allegedly an importer or a user of material that is under governmental, state, or municipal supervision. Drugs, chemicals, inflammables, and alcoholic beverages come within the purview of such licensing authorities. The investigator should familiarize himself with the occupations in the community which require licensing, and he should familiarize himself with the location of each of the bureaus charged with licensing specific operations. This knowledge will be of incalculable aid to any investigator.

The credit investigator may act for himself, or he may represent a credit reporting house, or he may be employed by the creditor. When the subject is approached, the investigator should identify himself in the usual way and state that he has called to obtain financial information with reference to the subject's business, preferably in the form of a financial statement.

Some investigators will leave a blank form for a financial statement to be executed by the subject and returned by mail. The reason for this is that the submission of a false financial statement by mail is a federal offense. While some states have statutory provisions providing that the submission in any manner of a false financial statement is a crime, the federal rule makes mailing one a mandatory crime.

The subject may ask why he should give any information about himself, what he has to gain by so doing. The answer should be that a supplier of merchandise or credit must know something about the potential customer and his business; that the more he knows about the subject, the sooner he will make a determination about extending the credit. The point should be emphasized that no good business—including the subject— would extend credit without knowing something about the debtor.

If the investigator is working on special assignment for the creditor, there may be a general inquiry as to why the creditor does not request the information himself instead of employing an intermediary. The answer should be that the creditor may not have the facilities to conduct individual investigations all over the country and that if he pursued such a course, costs would be higher and adjudications of credit risk slower. By sending a third-party credit investigator, who is an impartial, disinterested person, the matter is expedited for all concerned.

The subject should be interrogated about his business history and experience, the type of business he conducts, and the class of customers to whom he sells. The subject should be advised that this information is necessary in order to judge the amount of credit he is to receive.

If the blandishments of the investigator do not work and the subject refuses to divulge any information, no threats, implied or otherwise, should be made. Rather the subject should be advised politely that it is his privilege to refuse to give information, but in lieu thereof, the investigator will be forced to obtain the desired data from other sources. The fact should be brought out that every available extraneous source will be used, honestly and fairly, but that the information so received would be secondary and not so good as that flowing from the fountainhead—the subject himself. As a result, the picture to be presented to the creditors would not possibly be so good or so true as the one presented by the subject. The investigator may add that a refusal to submit information might hardly be construed as a proper foundation for a pleasant and mutually profitable relationship between the debtor and his creditors.

The field of collection is an outgrowth of the imperfections in the methods of extending credit. If the system of credit ratings were perfect, there would be no necessity for collection procedure. The good collector is the right arm of the finance company or credit house. He can often make or break his firm. His job is generally thankless and arduous but, under the present method of conducting business, very necessary. The collector must be courteous, diplomatic, tactful, and patient; and on the other hand, when necessary, he must be forward, aggressive, and belligerent. He must be a human paradox.

It is not the purpose of this chapter to detail the technicalities of credit and collection. Rather it is intended to clarify the weblike maze that connects every activity in these fields of business.

Success in the realm of collection is based in the main on the collector's ability as an investigator. The collection investigator must separate his debtors into several categories. The first class should include the debtor who is careless and whose account is small. It may also include the "close" debtor who has money in the bank but would rather keep it there than pay bills. In this category may also be placed the debtor who generally pays, but very slowly—the chronic "slowpoke." An appeal to pride will often exact results from these persons. Wheedling, coaxing, and patience will eventually be the means whereby collection will be effected.

The second group of debtors embraces the group that is slow due to temporary financial set-backs, such as illness, seasonal slumps in business, and so on. In such cases it is advocated that if collection cannot be effected immediately, a commitment be received, preferably in the form of a promissory note.

The third group of debtors includes those who, due to a combination of circumstances, verge on insolvency. Quick and effective means depending on the particular case in issue should be employed.

The fourth group embraces crooks and deliberate frauds. When this kind is detected, the debtor should be advised that his scheme is known. This often precipitates payment because there may be fear of criminal prosecution.

From a realistic standpoint, the collection investigator is interested in effecting collection rather than instituting criminal proceedings. In drastic cases, a draft should be drawn. It is often wise to advise the debtor of this action by letter first, because it is of course an unfriendly gesture. The draft may be sent to a bank in the debtor's vicinity or to the debtor's own bank. Often the debtor will be ashamed to dishonor a request made by a bank in his locality, especially if it is his own bank, because he will fear that his credit will be impaired. If the draft is presented to the debtor for collection and he does not honor it, the charges for such affirmative action are comparatively small.

Proper application of pressure may frequently result in a check being received from a debtor firm which is in financial difficulties and on the verge of bankruptcy or insolvency. The first thought of the collector is to have this check certified in view of the existing danger of financial upheaval which is momentarily expected in the debtor's firm. Frequently the bank refuses certification on the ground that insufficient funds are on deposit to cover the face amount of the check.

If the collector feels that the financial status of the debtor is such that anything realized on the check is "found money," the bank should be asked how much money is actually on deposit to the credit of the debtor. The difference between the amount on deposit and the amount of the check may be deposited by the creditor to the debtor's account, bringing the amount on deposit up to the sum listed on the check. In the same transaction the check may be certified. The amount originally on deposit therefore becomes salvage and recoverable. For example, if a collector is given a check for one thousand dollars by a debtor and the bank refuses certification because there is only five hundred dollars in the debtor's account, the collector may deposit five hundred dollars in cash to the debtor's account, if the circumstances warrant such action, bringing the balance up to the required one thousand dollars necessary toward effectuating certification.

Before this practice is employed, the collector should determine if there are any local laws which frown on such a procedure. Most jurisdicitons, however, consider it permissible in view of the bona fide debt owed as represented by the check.

It is frequently advisable for the investigator to call up the debtor on the telephone, following up with a registered letter and, if necessary, with a telegram. The latter has the ring of urgency. In any event, an effort should be made to exact a promise from the debtor so that when the time comes to keep the promise, he will be placed on the defensive if he fails to keep his word. Many investigators have accounts assigned to them to facilitate collection. There is no question that such procedure lends importance and standing to the transactions.

Frequently a collection investigator will wire a debtor's bank, merely inquiring if a judgment in a certain amount against the debtor is collectible. The bank will sometimes apprize the debtor of such an inquiry and, to avoid further embarrassment at his bank, payment is sometimes effected by this means.

It will often be found that there is more difficulty in obtaining payment from a debtor when the goods sold have been consumed or the money that was loaned has been spent. There is a natural reluctance to pay promptly for such indebtedness. There is no mysterious formula which facilitates collection in such cases. The investigator must use his best judgment and acumen in the light of the facts in the respective situations.

Often by intensive search in the various public bureaus, the investigator will unearth assets. He may find the debtor in possession of a car or a house. The successful collection is effected without the expense of a lawsuit, however, and finding assets does not mean that they can be seized and sold forthwith without due process of law to satisfy the claim. The good investigator finding assets will impress his knowledge of these facts upon the debtor. It may act as the persuasion to effect payment without litigation.

The investigator-collector has no hours. When necessary he should seek the debtor at his office. There is more of an inclination to pay under such circumstances because the continuing presence of a collector would prove embarrassing. A visit to the debtor's home at the dinner hour is often productive of results. The efficient investigator-collector knows his community, and he is familiar with pay days in the various factories and other places of business. His presence at the debtor's home just after he has been paid often proves productive.

Collection, like every other phase of investigation, produces its own problems which must be met with the solutions developed by the collector. Alertness and initiative are continually necessary to cope with the problems encountered. One of the thorniest problems besetting the collector-investigator is the lack of legal or technical proof of debt when suit is contemplated. Verbal or written demand may have been made and ignored. In preparing the matter for suit, there may be an insufficiency of satisfactory proof to substantiate the claim in the event it is disputed by the debtor.

A ruse that has been worked thousands of times successfully may still be tried. Let us assume the actual claim against a particular debtor is five hundred dollars, based on a verbal loan or other transaction where there is no written evidence of the debt. Letters to the debtor have gone unanswered and all other collection efforts have failed. The investigator may then send a telegram making one last demand for payment of the twelve-hundred-dollar debt. In practically every case the debtor, whether he pays or not, will write or wire back that the creditor is mistaken because he owes the creditor only five hundred dollars. Thus the debtor has admitted his liability in writing for the sum of five hundred dollars, and the plaintiff can proceed with suit without delay, as the evidence of indebtedness is now clear.

The collector-investigator should save all of his files and data pertaining to a particular debtor. If he has one claim against a particular debtor, the chances are that he will have several. The alert, efficient collector-investigator should know those statutory provisions in the state in which he operates pertaining to partners. He must be familiar with the rules of priority against partnership assets or the assets of the individual partners. He should know the rules pertaining to collection from corporations, especially those instances where personal liability may develop against officers, directors, or stockholders in such matters as wage claims. The potentiality of a claim against an individual officer, director, or stockholder may be used as a persuasive weapon to effect payment by the corporation.

The collector-investigator should be familiar with laws in his jurisdiction governing the enforceability of claims against infants and married women. The statutory provisions of a state which makes provisions for arrest, attachment, replevin, or garnishment of property must be known because these are the most potent weapons in consummating the collection.

When a collector-investigator visits the place of business of a debtor he should be observant of the stock in trade or other assets with the ultimate view of satisfying a judgment if all other methods of collection fail. Frequently, if a debtor is in business and is owed money by others, visits to the debtor's customers, ostensibly to verify their accounts with the debtor, may be a sufficient cause of embarrassment to the subject to result in payment of the claim being sought.

When the claim is assigned to the collection investigator, a check may be tendered to him in return for a general release. If the check is uncertified, the way to handle this transaction is for the investigator to give his release to the debtor *in* escrow. The debtor should give the investigator a receipt stating that the general release is received *in escrow*, in which status it will be held until the check clears the bank.

Income-tax returns are forbidden by law to be inspected by persons other than those specially designated by statute. However, if it is known who the auditor of a particular debtor is, an attempt may be made to inspect the retained copy in his possession. If this attempt is successful, a wealth of financial information about the debtor will become available.

The use of a personal advertisement in a newspaper will often result in locating a debtor. The advertisement is usually worded something like the following: "Am anxious to communicate with [insert the name of the person sought] on a very important matter." The advertisement is signed with a fictitious name and box number.

Some collection men are inveterate users of the decoy letter in an effort to locate the defaulting debtor. Several concerns are in the business of writing decoy letters. A letter is sometimes sent to the last known address of the debtor, or to a relative, to the effect that there is reason to believe the debtor might be an heir or participant in an estate. This method is more or less outmoded.

Dunning postal cards should not be sent because this practice is in conflict with the postal laws, although respectful reminders of current accounts owed are permissible. Extreme care should be exercised not to send any letters through the mails that are defamatory, threatening, scurrilous, or libelous. It is wise for the collector-investigator to familiarize himself thoroughly with that section of the postal laws dealing with permissible mailing matter.

If a defaulting debtor has filed a change of address in the post office and the investigator is unable to obtain it, there is still a means whereby he may ascertain the new address. Assuming that the name of the debtor is Joseph Doakes, the investigator may send a letter to Pete Flint, care of Joseph Doakes, at the latter's last known address. The name of Pete Flint is fictitious. The envelope must be marked "Deliver to Addressee Only." The letter should be sent by registered mail. The investigator, of course, is fully aware that the letter will be undelivered because Pete Flint is a fictitious name. When the letter goes to Joseph Doakes' first address, the postman or postal clerk will note the new address on the envelope, in conformity with the change of address notice. It will be sent to Pete Flint care of Joseph Doakes at the latter's present address, which will be marked on the envelope. When the letter is unaccepted by Pete Flint, because he does not exist, it will be returned to the sender—the investigator—and on the envelope will be the desired present address of Joseph Doakes.

Another method whereby the post office becomes the involuntary ally of the investigator makes use of the recent provision which allows a registered letter to be sent to any person, with a return made to the sender by the post office showing the address where the registered letter was actually delivered. There is an additional fee for this service which varies from established procedure only by giving the last address of the addressee on the return receipt in addition to the customary signature of the recipient of the communication.

The collector-investigator is not a popular man. This holds true not only insofar as the debtor is concerned, but with collateral leads as well. The collector-investigator should not disclose the details or the reason for his inquiries when such disclosures serve no purpose. While actual misstatements and deceit by the collector-investigator concerning his business are not advocated, it can do no harm if he identifies himself merely as an investigator if such a statement is in keeping with the ethical and legal requirements of the respective case. His onerous duties may create animus. To this reaction, he should present an imperturbable front. The old-style pugnacious collector who employed bullying and browbeating methods is a rarity today. Passions rouse the passions, and anger kindles anger. The clever collector-investigator uses methods that are much more subtle. The difference between the old-time loud-mouthed bullying collector and the modern collector is the difference between the beetle-browed, club-swinging police-man, whose chief joy was kicking in doors and bashing heads, and the studious, scientific crime detective of today.

The alert collection investigator should keep a vigilant eye on all unusual sales conducted by his firm's customers, espe-cially when the merchandise advertised for sale seems to be listed at a price which is below cost. This may presage bank-ruptcy or insolvency. A daily perusal of local newspapers is advisable, particularly those advertisements inserted by house-holders relating to items such as radios, refrigerators, furniture, or pianos. This alertness is especially important to time sales and installment investigators because such advertisements may often indicate the intention of a debtor to sell articles upon which full payment has not been made.

The collector in the installment field must be tenacious and persistent. The debtor will find it twice as hard to pay two installments at one time. The collector should use every reasonable means to prevent delinquency in any one payment. Promptness in meeting obligations is essential. While persist-ence is a virtue, if pressed too far it becomes a fault. No thorough collector should ever be loud or crude with a debtor when the latter is entertaining guests at his home. While a certain amount of moral persuasion and pressure is to be applied in some cases, intimidation should be implied and not exercised. The weapon to enforce collection is the fear on the part of the debtor that a certain line of conduct will be em-ployed by the collector. Once the line of conduct is actually employed, the collector has "shown his hand," with resulting bitterness on the part of the debtor, whose attitude may turn into vengefulness and spite. The easiest way for the debtor to show his animosity toward the collector is to refuse payment and to block the efforts of the collector with every conceivable obstacle.

In time-sales contracts, bitterness of the debtor because of the collector's actions may often result in a wilful destruction of the article purchased, so that when it is repossessed as a result of nonpayment its value is gone. Before any article is repossessed, a thorough check of the account should be made to verify the balance and to make sure no payments were made which were credited to another account. This will forestall future embarrassment in many instances. When the collateral is actually repossessed, painstaking examination should be made of its serial number and other identifying marks to see if it is the specific article which was sold. The identifying markings, insignia, or numbers of the repossessed article must coincide with those of the article sold. This is of paramount importance, and if this procedure is not rigorously adhered to in all cases, the investigating collector may soon find himself involved as a defendant in a conversion action.

Another "must" for the collector-investigator is thorough familiarity with his state's statutes pertaining to collection and procedure. Some jurisdictions now declare illegal the once prevalent collection practice of driving up to a debtor's home in a car or small panel truck which bore in glaring letters the legend that it belonged to a collection agency. Such practice is not advocated because it is crude, and in the long run harmful to the investigator because his integrity and methods are cheapened. This practice becomes known in a community, and the relationship of the collector and the debtor becomes questionable even before any personal contact is made.

Many states have peculiar quirks in their laws governing operation of inns, hotels, and lodging houses, and these provide that any items of personal property brought into a guest's room or apartment are subject to the primary innkeeper's lien for nonpayment of rent. In these instances, if an article is sold to a buyer on the installment plan or pursuant to a conditional bill of sale, the innkeeper's lien still takes precedence, unless, at the time of the sale the landlord or owner of the establishment is served with a copy of the agreement pertaining to the chattel brought to his premises. Knowledge of these statutory provisions is very important to the collector when the debtor lives in a hotel or lodging house. Some jurisdictions even carry the law so far as to state that if a friend of the guest visits him in his apartment and brings with him personal property which he leaves on the premises temporarily, such personal property becomes subject to the innkeeper's lien for unpaid rent or charges, even though the articles never were owned by the guest.

The letter is the foundation and the basis for initiating all credit collections. The style and tone of a letter depend very largely on its writer. There are, however, certain general principles which may be considered. When payment is not forthcoming on the due date, it is safe to rest on the assumption that the indebtedness has escaped the debtor's attention. This assumption may be only a fiction in the collector's mind, because he may know from past experiences with other accounts that this debtor is slow. Nevertheless, insofar as the current account is concerned, a short courteous reminder should be sent to the debtor. The tone should vary with succeeding letters until it is felt that friendly relations must be ruptured and a final letter containing the implications of drastic action is sent.

Letters should avoid excuses or apologies for making demand for payment. There is nothing to beg for if the money is due and should be paid. Excuses will weaken the creditor's position and encourage procrastination. When letters are written, the collector should have the complete file before him pertaining to the debtor's past history as an account. There may be an indication in the file as to the methods or processes which elicited favorable results on a prior occasion.

Discourteous, insulting, and provocative language will destroy the value and efficacy of the appeal contained in the letter. Written words carry a greater sting and authority than spoken words. A deliberately created animus will serve no purpose in collection, and a blend of dignity, courtesy, and firmness will go much further in attaining the results in dollars and cents which, after all, are the primary purpose of the collection investigator.

CHAPTER ELEVEN

BUSINESS HAZARDS AND PERSONNEL INVESTIGATION

ALMOST no person is unqualifiedly honest. Honesty depends on how much pressure is applied to provoke dishonesty. Our civilization makes it fitting, proper, and desirable to be honest. But the hard-won veneer of our culture, though shiny, is thin. By merely talking to a soldier who has spent a couple of months in combat in a steaming jungle it is possible to learn how easily the veneer of civilization is worn off. The investigator charged with protecting the interests of his employer against the potential dishonesty of employees should have a knowledge of those weaknesses and temptations that most beset humans.

Pressure manifests itself in various forms. An employee, honest by habit and inclination, may steal to provide for a child's operation, to pay a gambling debt, to win a woman's favor, to keep up with the Joneses, or for a myriad of other reasons. It would be foolhardy to try to draw a line of demarcation showing how much pressure a person can withstand in the form of need, provocation, revenge, or temptation in a particular individual's case. Inherent strength in a person may be whittled down and worn away by the continual temptations placed in his path or by the lack of watchfulness exercised over him, giving him the belief that his dishonesty will remain undetected.

Conversely, inherent weakness will not be supported, nor

will it be allowed to manifest itself, if watchfulness and vigilance over the individual are continually practiced and temptation is removed from his path. The writer knows that he will be accused of cynicism and skepticism for his belief that every living person has a breaking point in his principles, morals, or honesty. Many readers of this book will vehemently disagree with this premise.

It is difficut to believe, however, that a person on the verge of death from starvation will stop to inquire about the ownership of a loaf of bread found by the side of the road. To make the pressure still stronger, is it possible to believe that a parent would not take this loaf for his starving child?

Pressure rears its head in many forms, and it manifests itself in varying degrees which must be considered by the investigator in the light of the degree of resistance to stress possessed by the specific person concerned. What may be considered overwhelming temptation in one case may be resisted in another because of the inherent strength of the subject.

There comes a time, however, when pressure may be so overpowering, and the ability to resist it so puny that the succumbing of the individual to this influence becomes almost a matter of reflex action. The will and desire to resist become negligible. It is as if a person, by the exercise of almost superhuman will power, should attempt suicide by holding his breath. After a short time elapses without breathing, unconsciousness will result. As soon as the senses leave the body, however, the person starts breathing again because will and intent have fled, and the instinctive desire of the body to live manifests itself, unhampered by the machinations of reason.

When the personnel investigator considers the merits of an applicant for a key position, he will generally consider the factors of judgment, loyalty, character, and integrity, in addition to ability. The suggestions listed elsewhere in this book will be of help in procuring a composite picture of a prospective employee. Past employment, business and professional history, ability, and qualifications should be examined. In addition, if the applicant has been in the military service, his Army or Navy specialties may be procured from the Demobilized Records Branch of the Adjutant General's Department or from the Bureau of Naval Personnel.

Habits, reputation, character, financial standing, and special achievements should be ascertained. Bankruptcy and credit records should be examined, and a checkup for a criminal record should never be overlooked. If the applicant has ever been in business, former employees may supply considerable unadulterated information not obtainable elsewhere.

The interview with the applicant, though conducted in a friendly and informal manner, should be of soul-searching scrutiny. Ambitions, hobbies, and recreations should be discussed with complete thoroughness. Law infractions, no matter how minor, should be subjected to inquiry. Previous addresses, family background, and credit difficulties are subjects to cover. These matters may seem very minor, but they are of extreme importance in determining the character of the applicant. If the statements as to minor matters are investigated and turn out to be false, it is an important element of evaluation, even though the matters which were the subject of the investigation are in themselves unimportant.

It is of far greater value to the employer to use preventive measures when hiring an applicant than punitive methods after the employee turns out to be dishonest. There are certain psychological aspects that operate as a precaution against dishonesty. If employees are fingerprinted and photographed, it tends to make them crime-conscious and it tends to create in them an awareness of apprehension and punishment. The use of a bonding company's indemnity bond will also place the employee on notice that a third party, perhaps not as under-standing or forgiving as the employer, is in the picture.

Frequently when an employee is caught in a dishonest act, the employer must make the unenviable decision whether to prosecute or merely discharge the employee. From a realistic standpoint, there is no greater deterrent to the commission of future crimes by the employees of any organization than the exposure and successful prosecution of one of their number.

Some firms keep suggestion boxes easily accessible to all employees. If a suggestion toward the betterment of the firm is acceptable, a reward may be paid to the holder of the stub bearing the same number as the suggestion, which is unsigned. This means of conveying information to an employer is fre-quently used by employees who choose to remain anonymous by retaining the stub when they report instances of improper conduct or dishonesty practiced by other employees. The per-sonnel investigator should encourage the use of suggestion boxes as a possible source of information pertaining to irreg-ularities.

The use of microfilm machines is rapidly gaining headway in many firms. Every bill, voucher, draft, check, invoice, receipt, and purchase order is photographed in miniature by the micro-film process and filed in the firm's vaults. The knowledge that such replicas of business transactions exist permanently tends to act as a deterrent to the destruction, mutilation, addition, or alteration of records in furtherance of illegal schemes developed by dishonest employees.

One of the troublesome problems confronting employers is that of the dishonest employee who has formed another com-pany which sends spurious bills to the employer for which the dishonest employee secures payment by his employer. The employee may go to a neighboring city and rent space for an office. He is the sole owner of a sham firm, generally filing a trade-name certificate under an alias. Stationery for the new firm is printed, and invoices are sent to the company for which the dishonest employee works. The scheming employee is usually in a position to make payment on behalf of the organization employing him, or he may be operating with a confederate. The payments are made to the fictitious firm and deposited to its account, later being drawn out in the form of cash by the same employee under his alias. This method of defalcation is very difficult to detect.

The best practical manner of investigating this type of suspected violation is to have a credit report made on the employer's creditors. It may sound inane to check the credit of the company which is the alleged seller, but only by this means may its component structure and existing suspicious circumstances become known.

In instances of recurring thefts in offices, factories, schools, gymnasiums, hospitals, meeting places, and theaters suitable traps may be laid by the investigator for the malefactor, especially when it is believed to be an "inside job." Thefts of this nature generally consist of pilfering in cloakrooms, lavatories, and dressing rooms. They may also embrace the forcing of desks, lockers, and cabinets. Decoy pocketbooks, jewels, or other valuable articles may be placed in obvious places so as to invite pilfering. Brilliant, slow-drying dyes may be applied to the article which will immediately stain the thief's hands. Other so-called "dry dyes" will not immediately stain, but the dampness of the skin due to perspiration will soon bring the color out. Other chemicals constitute the "non-apparent" dyes which have luminous qualities not discernible to the naked eye. Ultraviolet rays will detect the luminescence even after the hands are washed.

Situations may arise where the thief will be caught with the telltale incriminating dye on his hands, yet the stolen money cannot be found on his person or the premises. In these instances, it should be determined if there is a mail box or letter drop in the building. Many sneak thieves carry a stamped addressed envelope on their persons. After a theft, in order not to be found with the incriminating evidence, the stolen money is placed in the envelope and immediately mailed by the thief to himself.

If an employer suspects that his desk is being tampered with, he may employ a ruse long used successfully. Half of a bill of substantial denomination, lightly sprinkled with fine powder, may be left in the desk drawer. The powder should bring fingerprints out in glaring relief. Any other object of value might be stolen and thus render the experiment valueless. An object without value would probably not be handled. This half bill by its very nature invites attention, and after it receives the attention it merits by being handled, it is returned to its former place, bearing the fingerprints of the sneak thief.

There is a prevailing belief that half of a bill of any denomination is valueless, giving rise to the underworld practice of paying half of a fee in advance on an illegal assignment by tendering half of a bill. When the unlawful job is completed, the other half of the same bill is delivered. It is the underworld's bilateral contract. The good investigator should realize that no belief is more fallacious, because one half of a genuine bill of any denomination, in legible form, will be redeemed by the Treasury Department at one half the face value of the bill.

An investigator employed by a firm selling valuables such as jewelry should be wary of those sales whereby items are to be delivered C.O.D., especially to hotels or business addresses. Even residences are not immune from this abuse because criminals will sublease a house or an apartment solely for the purpose of defrauding the businessman. When the articles are delivered, care should be used to see that they are not removed from the presence of the messenger until payment is made. The articles may be taken to another room on pretext of unwrapping or examination, or for the ostensible purpose of getting the money. The "buyer" will then vanish with the loot.

Some package thieves will follow a delivery boy from the employer's place of business in order to note the place of delivery on the parcel. Other package thieves will casually note and record the addresses on packages as they are loaded on a delivery truck. The thief will hurry to the designated address and wait in the doorway of the apartment house or office building for the messenger. When the messenger arrives, the thief will identify himself as the consignee, and ask for the package from "Mason's" store, berating the employee in the meantime for lateness of delivery. Employees should be properly trained and instructed how to cope with these hazards.

A gadget which should be discouraged is the miniature license plate worn on a key ring, ostensibly to effect return of car keys that have been lost. Many employees, working as drivers, carry such identification, and if the key chain is lost or stolen, the thief may merely go to the nearest parking lot to pick out a vehicle bearing the same number as the miniature, climb in, and drive away.

Shoplifting is a double-edged hazard confronting the investigator. It presents not only the problem concerning the intrinsic loss of the stolen merchandise but the delicate issue of handling shoplifting problems due to the danger of suits arising from false arrests.

Some shoplifters operate in groups of two or three. One may engage the attention of the saleslady and perhaps arrange to buy a cheap dress. While the saleslady removes the garment to the alteration room, the confederate may filch an expensive gown and hide it under her dress or coat, or casually go to the nearest lady's room, where she will don the stolen article. Care and vigilance should be exercised in all retail departments contiguous or adjacent to rest rooms. Dishonest employees, desiring to steal articles from their employers, also use the rest room to attain their illegal schemes. An article nonchalantly thrown over the arm of an employee may be quickly taken into the rest room and donned under the outer clothing.

Greater success is attained by the shoplifter in the winter season when heavy outer clothing is worn. An umbrella or large shopping bag is often carried. Articles are "accidentally" dropped into these receptacles and the shoplifter, when questioned, will protest shrilly and loudly that the items fell into the containers without her knowledge.

The danger of false arrest must be kept continually in the mind of the investigator operating in retail establishments. No overt act should be attempted against any suspected shoplifter unless the facts upon which the action is predicated are as certain as are humanly possible to determine. Clever ruses are employed by some persons in an effort to make themselves appear as shoplifters when, in fact, they are not. The most prevalent one is the case of a customer who comes to a crowded store and buys an article, making payment for it and obtaining a receipt. The customer leaves, but comes back later with the same article, laying it down again in a place where similar objects are sold. After a few moments of puttering about the customer will pick up the article previously bought and paid for and walk away with it. The assumption will arise naturally that a theft is being committed. If an arrest should be made in this instance, the store would be in a very embarrassing situation indeed in view of the prior valid sale substantiated by a sales slip.

Potential buyers who make repeated visits to inspect specific costly articles in a shop should be isolated for special, careful scrutiny. Sometimes the potential buyer will bring a woman companion along and ask her if the article meets with her approval. In the meantime he has had the opportunity to examine and inspect the article thoroughly, and from his knowledge of the object he is able to manufacture an imitation.

The imitation is sometimes actually brought to the shop and compared with the original. Finally, when the imitation is perfected, the violator will effect a switch, exchanging the spurious one for the genuine. Several days may pass before the crime is discovered.

It is a matter of common knowledge that many employees will simulate burglaries or thefts to cover their own defalcations. The average employee about to simulate a crime seldom has a correct idea of a burglar's method. He therefore fails to avoid ordinary pitfalls. Broken windows will be found broken from the inside; there will be thick coatings of undisturbed dust on transoms, although this means is the only apparent way of entrance; there will be no trace of dirt or moisture on the floor of the burgled premises, even though it has rained or snowed during the period of the alleged burglary. Investigation may disclose other signs pointing to a feigned, rather than an actual crime.

A theft which proves to be genuine should still be scrutinized closely for the actual amount of the loss. Often greater damage will be claimed than was actually incurred. An employee might perpetrate the crime for personal aggrandizement at the expense of his employer, and frequently an employer will employ this subterfuge to obtain a larger settlement from his indemnity company.

The professionally dishonest employee will sometimes obtain employment under a false name and fictitious social security number with the plan fixed in his mind to consummate the crime before the Social Security authorities discover the falsehood. Such a dishonest employee will generally wait for the day before a holiday or week end to make good his "killing" and then disappear. Again the emphasis is to be placed on greater care in hiring.

The checker, weighmaster, or shipping clerk is in a position to do great harm by uncontrolled deliveries of merchandise to a confederate. The dishonest driver will deliberately spend an unreasonably long time in a restaurant or saloon while an accomplice unloads and steals the contents of the truck.

Hotels have an unusual share of perplexing dilemmas. In addition to the problems presented by dishonest employees, the professional hotel thief registering as a guest becomes a formidable obstacle to the management of a hotel.

The methods of hotel thieves vary. One will wander about the halls until he sees a room being cleaned. He will keep this room under surveillance until the maid leaves for towels and sheeting or other supplies. The thief will dash in and grab anything of value in the room. Sometimes a confederate may engage the maid in conversation for a short time until the actual filcher has had the opportunity to leave the floor. The maid generally does not discover the theft, and a good start is obtained by the violators.

Another hotel thief may observe the habits of guests and note when they are out of their rooms. He may make his entry by a passkey or by any one of a number of keys in his possession obtained by prior registration.

Hotel managements should instruct all the employees to be on the alert constantly for any guest who tinkers with the lock on the door of his room. Careful surveillance should be kept of such a guest, even if he explains that his door stuck, or that he oiled the lock or is unlimbering its stiffness.

The fact remains that the most troublesome hotel thief is the one who is able to procure a passkey that will open any of the rooms. Often such thieves will attempt to remove the lock to take it to a locksmith for the manufacture of a passkey, or a wax impression will be made of the inner mechanism. The thief who uses passkeys will sometimes borrow one from a bellboy whom he has been tipping liberally on the pretext of opening his own room because he forgot his key, and with the promise of returning the key immediately. The key is kept just long enough to make a wax impression. The thefts will not generally take place at that time, but after a suitable interval has expired during which the malefactor has checked out and returned to the hotel in possession of a passkey.

A hotel should endeavor to have the keys to its rooms kept in compartments not visible to anyone in the lobby. Many hotel thefts are accomplished by thieves who observe a guest leave the hotel, casually dropping his room key on the desk as he goes by. The thief will shortly ask for the key to this particular room. In busy hotels the management often is not familiar with its guests, and as a result the key will be handed over without question.

Frequently thieves will look over the room numbers to see which box contains a key, indicating that the guest in a particular room is out. The key will be requested and the theft consummated.

A hotel is like a woman. The chief asset of its business life is its good name. A hotel's good name and reputation are maintained by a consistent, active preventive program. Like a woman whose chastity is impugned, the accusation of immorality is tantamount to a conviction. A hotel investigator must be the acme of diligence and tact in ferreting out and frustrating the efforts of those persons who would exploit the guests.

In hotels particularly great care should be exercised before any overt act is committed by the management which might reflect on the integrity, character, or chastity of any of its guests. Very frequently a false arrest or unjustified "scene" provoked by the management has resulted in millions of dollars in damages being assessed against hotels. The hotel investigator or house detective is the insurance for an organization to be kept out of such involvements.

Any number of cases are on record where the management forced entry into a room occupied by a woman who was be-

lieved to be entertaining a man for immoral purposes. In some
instances the hotels were badly mistaken because the man and
the woman were married. It is believed although not yet
proved, that some women will deliberately provoke a raid on
their rooms by their actions, and the men found with them
will be their husbands. This makes a very good case against the
hotel and is almost always good for a favorable judgment unless collusion or conspiracy can be shown.

A favorite scheme, the method of which is almost identical
in most cases, is employed intermittently by thieves using a
hotel as a background. A well-dressed man will check into a
hotel and pay all his bills and charges promptly. On a Saturday
afternoon when the banks are closed he will enter a nearby
jewelry shop—preferably one in the hotel building. He will
purchase an item of jewelry for perhaps five hundred dollars
and tender a check in payment, listing the hotel as a credit
reference. The hotel will be called to verify the credit of the
person, and because of the guest's excellent credit history, the
report will be good. The purchaser will then return to the
hotel and request that his bill be made up because he is checking out. The guest will attempt to sell the article recently purchased, and he will approach the bartender, the desk clerk, or
any available employee, asking about fifty dollars for the piece
of jewelry. The guest will seem to be in a hurry and anxious
to consummate the sale. Finding a buyer at the bargain price
is not difficult, and the sale is usually closed in a short time,
and the employee lets his purchase be known.

The hotel management, which has just received a call from
the jeweler relative to the credit of the guest, smells a rat and
usually notifies the jewelry firm that the article it just sold for
five hundred dollars has been resold for fifty dollars. The
obvious inference is that the check tendered in payment is no
good. In a case of this kind the jeweler cannot verify the
validity of the check because the banks are closed. In a frantic

endeavor to apprehend the person who is about to leave town and who apparently has just defrauded the firm with a bad check, it does the obvious. The firm has the guest arrested.

The prisoner languishes in jail until Monday morning, when he is arraigned for hearing on account of the alleged bad check. But the blackest of surprises confronts the jeweler, for the bank representative will testify that the five-hundred-dollar check was good, and that a check for a much greater sum would have been honored. The erstwhile guest has deliberately created a set of circumstances which gives rise to the belief that he had given a bad check and instigated his own arrest so that he can bring a suit for false arrest.

There is not an industry nor an establishment in existence which does not have to contend with risks peculiar to its own sphere of activity. The investigator must be cognizant of all the ramifications in his chosen field. A railroad or steamship company investigator may have problems similar to those arising in hotels, complicated by baggage thefts, accidents, integrity of personnel, malicious damage to property presenting a safety hazard, and "dead beats."

A claims investigator for an indemnity company is sometimes called an "honesty engineer." Systems which can be used as safeguards against thefts are available. For instance, valuable stock may be placed in a separate enclosure under strict supervision, and a perpetual inventory may be maintained by the use of duplicate sales slips. It is often advisable to bring in a third party such as an "honesty engineer" to make a survey of a firm's precautionary measures against theft. Employers, like many others who live very close to their immediate problems, sometimes cannot see the forest for the trees. An outside person with a fresh perspective may detect glaring flaws without undue effort.

Risks of losses through dishonesty of employees have become greater in recent years than at any previous time. War displacement of personnel and the upheaval in industry have resulted in the hiring of many persons for positions of trust who would not ordinarily have been considered. Understaffed offices resulting from labor shortages have also materially aided the prospective embezzler.

Platitudes are dangerous rules to follow because they can be fitted to any situation. But the old saying "there is safety in numbers" has no truer application than when applied to a group of employees. The larger the business, the more safeguards may be employed.

An indemnity investigator functioning as an "honesty engineer" should be on the alert for certain danger signs. Undue slowness in hitherto normal paying accounts or a sudden unexplained increase in accounts receivable may indicate a defalcation. Unusual differences between the actual and perpetual inventory records may point to a theft of merchandise or fraudulent payment to fictitious persons. Unexplained, sudden diminution of profits is a factor for consideration.

The good investigator who surveys a business develops an intuitive "feel" of particular situations and people. The mere presence of an investigator often causes the guilty person to betray himself in some fashion.

An advisable safeguard in an organization is that of compelling each employee to take a vacation at stated intervals. Flexible rotation of duties is also advocated. It is not advisable for the periods of rotation to be fixed too far in advance because regularity of rotation may apprize employees in advance what jobs they will fill. Such prior knowledge may be encouragement toward collusion.

Countersigning of checks by a responsible official should be required in all firms. The countersigning official should be impressed with the fact that this function is not casual nor perfunctory. Periodic special verification of bank balances should be made, either by letter or telegram. Some embezzling clerks have procured blank bank statements and filled them out fraudulently in such a way as to reflect a larger balance than actually existed. Periodic statements of account are mailed by many firms requesting confirmation of the amount owed.

Physical inventories should be taken by someone other than the custodian of the merchandise. Inventory checkers should also be rotated. It is strongly advocated that all mail be opened by a trusted official or employee, someone other than the individuals charged with processing the communications.

Another important safeguard is the proviso that no employee may cash checks payable to the firm. All banks with which the firm does business should be notified that checks payable to it must be deposited. All checks received by a firm should be marked "For deposit only" before endorsement. If business exigencies are such that exceptions to this rule become necessary, certain specified persons should be authorized to cash checks, and the banks should be notified in writing of the names of the persons so authorized, together with specimens of their handwriting.

Firm checks should be executed by a check writing machine which perforates the paper. In the absence of such a machine, the entire space on the line of the check providing for the insertion of the amount should be used. This will prevent the "raising" of the check by the addition of other letters or symbols. If the space cannot be entirely filled, a line should be drawn through the unused portion to preclude the insertion of extraneous writing in that space.

Payment for materials purchased should be made by check as far as possible, because this procedure will discourage a dishonest employee from paying himself or a confederate for fictitious merchandise.

A common means of embezzlement is by understating the amount of sales. If it is feasible, this type of summary should be prepared by an individual employee charged with this specific task. Alertness should be exercised against pay-roll padding, which is one of the most common forms of concealing systematic embezzlements. No specific precaution is advanced because the methods and procedures in effecting pay-roll preparation vary considerably with most organizations.

The foregoing suggestions will tend to minimize losses by detecting irregularities at an early time. Even before losses are suspected, it is good policy to conduct regular honesty surveys. The inspections should be apparent and obvious, yet general enough to keep the exact details from the employees. The scope of the examinations should be wide enough to convey the impression to each employee that the full line of his duties will be embraced by the survey. This is one of the more important measures available to employers to create an effective barrier of preventive forces against the outcropping of dishonesty.

CHAPTER TWELVE

INSURANCE

THE INSURANCE ADJUSTER

THE failure to discover important evidence and the drawing of erroneous conclusions are not always due to lack of industry on the part of the insurance investigator. They are often due to lack of knowledge and experience. It is hoped that the foregoing pages have given the insurance adjuster a proper perspective of the investigative facilities available to him. No single book can embrace the entire field of insurance. The tenuous investigative trail, however, may be blazed through mazes of unknown and uncharted fields. The investigator's unfamiliarity with any sphere of technical activity does not of itself present a barrier to him provided he is a capable, experienced prober. A good invesigator possesses the keys of knowledge that will unlock the doors to many problems.

Whenever monetary gain or loss will result from settling insurance disputes, the investigator will meet with incredibly varying and contradictory reactions to the same set of facts. An accurate and scientific presentation of the facts can be attained only by work, perseverance, patience, and the application of the newest methods born of the experiences of others.

The insurance investigator must always be aware of the fact that when he appears before a jury, he represents "big business." To the average group of ordinary men who comprise a jury, an insurance company is an ogre, an impersonal commercial giant. As a result, if it is known that an insurance company is involved, its representative, the investigator, may be regarded with a jaundiced eye. He should seek to overcome such prejudice by his conduct, demeanor, and knowledge of the subject matter of his investigation. While the insurance investigator is a gatherer of facts, to be presented by counsel, the attorney cannot operate intelligently in many cases without the aid and co-operation of the investigator. The jury knows this and will consequently react to the case by its judgment of the investigator. Every effort should be made to keep the insurance company from being mentioned or involved in the picture in any way. The investigator should never take a statement on the company's stationery, nor should he mention the company in a statement he takes from a witness. These statements might be used in evidence, and the fact that an insurance company is involved is immediately obvious.

The good insurance investigator must know his territory, with special emphasis on those areas that are breeding places of accidents such as railroad crossings, dangerous intersections, and blind corners. Depending on the nature of his special investigations, he should be familiar with the known "fences" used by the jewel, fur, automobile, silverware, and auto accessory thieves. The investigator should know the identity of suspected and potential arsonists, and his informants should keep him advised of firms which, on the verge of insolvency, might welcome a fire loss.

The investigator should be familiar with the identity of professional "floppers" or "repeaters" in simulated accidents. He must have a speaking knowledge of the underlying principles on which casualty insurance is founded, and of the divisions of its activities, together with a thorough knowledge of the operating problems of the division in which he is currently employed. While a "pinch hitter" or "trouble-shooting" investigator can be, and is, continually assigned from one type of investigation to another, the well-grounded investigator is the backbone of sound investigation in the field of insurance.

The insurance investigator should also possess certain tools of his trade. He should always carry portable instruments for measurement and observation necessary in procuring relevant and material evidence in a scientific manner.

The investigator is the eyes and ears for the company in advising them of any factors which increase the hazard. These factors will not always drop easily into his lap. He must go after them, using the various means at his disposal, some of which are described in this book, in order to effectively assure a continuous flow of accurate information through his own personal sources of information.

Special care should be taken when questioning a witness to test the accuracy of his affirmative statements. It is not meant that the veracity of the witness should be questioned, but his ability to make an accurate analysis of an occurrence should be checked. For instance, a witness may say that two minutes elapsed between the time certain events occurred. What the witness means by a two-minute interval should be verified. He might actually mean thirty seconds or five minutes. Or the witness might say that a particular estimated distance was twenty feet. This should also be checked to determine the witness's concept of distance, times, colors, amounts, shades, and speeds. The investigator's witness may otherwise turn out to be a sad disappointment.

Nervousness, pain, anxiety, anger, excitement, grief, or ulterior motive should also be considered when the verbal portrayal of events is obtained from the witness. Descriptions by witnesses of automobile accidents, for instance, are often warped, and the product of their impressionable imaginations has its basis in emotion rather than in actual, factual observation. For example, if an automobile driver under the influence of liquor injures a pedestrian, bystanders will invariably say that the driver was proceeding at a high rate of speed, even if this were not the fact.

The adjuster should know the reasons inspiring the performance of his duties. Insurance, briefly defined, means that a number of persons, each of whom is subject to a similar risk of loss, contribute to a common fund to compensate those in the group who actually suffer such a loss. It is an arrangement whereby small certain payments are substituted for large uncertain ones. The word *policy*—derived from the Italian *polizza* meaning contract—means the agreement in writing to indemnify the assured, to make good to him certain losses suffered. The conditions pursuant to which compensatory payment for the losses sustained will be made are clearly set forth in the policy. Whether a policy be for burglary and theft, fire, personal injury or property damage, death, health, accident, workmen's compensation, and so on, the adjuster must have a full and intimate knowledge of its contents in order to determine if it provides proper coverage. This is the guarantee against specific losses incurred under certain conditions as provided by the terms of the policy.

It is wise to differentiate between the insurance company's adjuster and its broker. While the adjuster is the employee and representative of a particular company, the broker does not enjoy this status. The latter maintains his own offices, and he generally does not confine his efforts to procuring business for any one specific insurance company; instead, he places his customer's business with the company giving the best terms and the most protection. The broker's interests are usually inclined toward the assured and not toward the company because, in fact, the assured is his client. Investigators are required constantly, therefore, to probe claims urged by the broker which are outside the scope of a policy.

Since most policies are written through brokers, most claims are made through them. Investigators should realize fully the part played by brokers in filing claims. The good insurance adjuster has brokers in his area catalogued for reliability, dishonesty, exaggeration, integrity, or the propensity toward sheer fabrication.

If the trend of an investigation leads the adjuster to suspect that a crime has been committed, it is advisable to inform the proper prosecuting authorities. Only violations that can be definitely proved should be revealed to the officials. The investigator should state, when turning over such a case, that he feels it to be his duty to divulge such information. No request for an arrest or indictment should ordinarily be made by the insurance adjuster; such decisions should be left to the prosecuting officials.

In interviewing an assured person who is a suspect, no betrayal of suspicion should be made on the first contact. No accusation or aspersion on the assured's character should ever be made in the presence of witnesses unless the insurance adjuster and his company wish to place themselves in the position of being vulnerable to suits for slander.

The insurance adjuster who works on numerous cases simultaneously, especially when he has a large geographical area to cover, should keep a comprehensive record of his appointments, which are often arranged in advance. There is no single factor which turns a witness against the investigator so much as a broken appointment. Some investigators use a novel reminder, especially when traveling, by mailing penny postal cards to themselves as reminders of appointments.

One of the leading adjustment companies lists the following as qualifications for an insurance adjuster: judgment, self-control, cheerfulness, orderliness, punctuality, industry, initiative, reliability, inquisitiveness, co-operation, and loyalty. While so much virtue may merit a halo, these traits are nevertheless necessary to attain status as a good insurance adjuster.

Insurance investigation is an arduous field, and it is a jealous profession that brooks no rivals. That it is fast becoming an activity of recognized professional standing is indicated by the slow but powerful movement to license accredited insurance adjusters and place them under state supervision. Every insurance adjuster should obtain copies of questions and answers for examinations that have been given and the requirements for taking such tests in those states already possessing prescribed licensing provisions for insurance adjusters. The information they contain will be of invaluable assistance to any insurance investigator.

The claim agent representing a company is its most important contact with the assured. Up to the time of the assured's first claim, he has been told only what the company will do. The duty of the insurance claim agent is to fulfill those promises in fairness to the assured and to the company alike. If a claim is made in good faith, and the investigator performs his duties properly, conflicts can generally be resolved without resorting to litigation. The insurance investigator should remember that the assured and all those like him collectively cause his company to function. The assured's problems and demands, therefore, should be considered sympathetically because in the average case the problems of the company and those of the assured are identical, and a relationship based on mutual confidence should exist. If fraud or bad faith is found, these general rules of policy of course do not apply.

The insurance investigator must always remember that he is dealing with the human element. Evidence may sometimes be obtained by the mere asking. In other instances, it must be pried from a reluctant and opposing mind. The investigator must exercise all his wiles, experience, and ability to create those necessary impressions upon a person to precipitate a flow of information. An application of the science of investigation should be directed by good judgment. The character of the witness should be analyzed with the view of stimulating dominant traits in order to effect the desired action.

Certain general traits among people should be considered. Racial strains of the witnesses, if known to the investigator, should be respected insofar as traditional or religious holidays and customs are concerned. The investigator will have little success if he attempts to interview an orthodox Jew on Yom Kippur or a devout Catholic on Good Friday.

Most men, even those in the lowliest and humblest positions, do not like to be dominated or treated as inferiors. Any manifestation of condescension or superiority on the part of the investigator will be countered with resentment and obstinacy by the witness. The investigator must remember that all men must be met and treated as equals, as human beings, and not as impersonal, insensate objects. An insensate object cannot be fashioned to conform with any personality, while the human mind can be sympathetically molded to fit the contours of the adjuster's intellect.

ARSON

Every day in the United States there are fifteen hundred fires exacting a daily toll of thirty deaths. Investigation in the field of arson was accelerated by World War II primarily because of "Operation Hotfoot." This wartime army project, which resulted in the development of the jellied gasoline incendiary bomb, actually built the counterparts of German and Japanese towns in the Utah desert. These communities were complete reproductions, using even the type of material used in German and Japanese structures, streets, furniture, and plumbing. The Japanese mats used were authentic furnishings from the homes of displaced Japanese on the west coast.

As a result of the detailed experiments, hitherto unknown facts were disclosed which are of invaluable assistance in trailing down arson suspects. It was ascertained that there is a definite relationship between kinds of wood and their burning properties. For instance, it takes forty-six seconds to kindle a standard piece of spruce, whereas it takes one hundred and sixty-two seconds for a piece of hard maple to ignite. When a suspected arson case is investigated, the type of wood in the structure or vehicle burned should be noted for possible future scientific investigation. Similarly, wood thickness should be noted because of the greater fire resistance in woods of greater mass.

The weather and season should be noted also, because water content in wood is an important element in the scientific determination of its burning propensities. Water content changes from season to season, and a moisture-saturated structure during a wet summer or fall presents a different fire hazard from the tinder-dry building after a rainless summer. The time element in an arson case may be fixed by consideration of these and similar points.

"Operation Hotfoot" also disclosed that massive furniture is more resistant to fire, than light or so-called "modern" furniture. Popular impression notwithstanding, a coat of paint, if not fresh, is better protection against fire than a bare surface.

The best starting point for an arsonist is in the line of the eaves of an attic, and fires known to have their inception at this place should be the object of special scrutiny. The investigator should determine if any objects in the burned structure had been made heat-resistant by chemicals. Examination of such articles also may shed considerable light on the time the fire began.

It is difficult to obtain a conviction in an arson case because in most instances the fire has destroyed the traces of implicating evidence, so that often the case must be built up on circumstantial evidence. The laws pertaining to arson vary somewhat in most states, but the existence of the fire and its incendiary origin must be proved in all states.

The proof that a fire actually occurred must be submitted. Mere scorching, discoloration, staining, or smoking of a building is not a fire within the purview of the law. There must be some burning. Charring, so that the fiber of the wood is destroyed, or its identity changed, is considered burning. It is not necessary for the fire to do great damage for the origin to be considered arson. It is sufficient that fire existed.

The easiest way for the investigator to prove the existence of fire is to present, in open court, a board from the building allegedly fired so that judicial determination may be made whether it has been burned or not. A photograph of the burned structure or vehicle may also be presented to depict more graphically than words can describe the nature of the damage.

In addition to showing the existence of the fire, it must be shown that it was started as the result of a wilful act by some person. Evidence must be presented that the fire was of incendiary origin. All fires are presumed to be of accidental origin as long as no proof to the contrary exists. It is therefore necessary to introduce positive evidence to overcome this presumption and to prove the corpus delicti.

The evidence may be procured in various ways. Threats made by the accused to the owner or occupant of the burned property or adjoining premises may be shown. So may ill feeling or other evidences of motive. Possession or purchase of inflammable material by the accused may also be shown. Any prior conduct tending to show the intention of the accused to defraud the insurer may be submitted to establish a motive. Some of the more common motives are revenge, jealousy, economic gain attained either by defrauding an insurer or eliminating a competitor, race or religious prejudice, and the covering up of a crime.

If openings have been made for the spread of the flames, it may be shown that the accused had the tools to make the openings. If cork stopples were used to plug the sprinklers of a factory, it may be proved the accused had a supply of cork, or the stopples were set in a place accessible to the suspect. If a fire were set by a contrivance peculiarly adapted for incendiary purposes, it may be shown that the accused had a workshop and the means and the ability to construct such a device.

There is rarely a case where a setting of the fire has been witnessed. The corpus delicti must almost always be proved by any of the myriad means presented through the medium of circumstantial evidence.

In addition to the fires occurring because of the motives listed above, there is the not inconsiderable number set by pyromaniacs. This inner compulsion or obsession which compels the perpetrator to set a fire is a neurosis which is generally an objective sympton of a mental disorder. The compelling obsession may be to see fire engines race or to commit self-mutilation. Some members of volunteer fire departments have been known to set fires in order to wear their uniforms. Some sadists deliberately set fire to barns, warrens, chicken houses, or woods just for the pleasure they receive in burning animals alive. Whatever the reason behind the acts, pyromaniacs are difficult to detect because of the absence of conventional motives and the penchant to work alone. When a series of fires of unknown origin breaks out under similar circumstances, such as in unoccupied or isolated structures or in particular portions thereof, it is safe to presume that a pyromaniac is loose in the neighborhood.

In establishing responsibility for a fire, it is not necessary for the investigator to show that the accused set a fire with his own hand nor that the suspect was present. It is sufficient to show that he procured another to commit the crime or otherwise aided or abetted in the commission of the act. To establish the corpus delicti, the investigator may seek out collateral issues, such as evidence that the efforts of firemen would be retarded. This is sometimes shown by nails in the streets leading to the scene of the fire, broken mains or plugs, drained pools or reservoirs in rural areas, or obstacles to fire equipment such as the apparently accidental breakdown of a truck in a driveway.

The removal before the fire of valuable furniture, stock, or merchandise can be shown. The absence of the accused's family on a visit in a neighboring town during the time of the fire may be a vital point. Every fact and circumstance which may throw light on the motivations of the defendants in the case may be admitted in evidence.

The financial condition of a suspect should always be thoroughly examined, because indications may be found that he needed to realize funds quickly. Frequently account books are sought to be destroyed when they might have been the basis for fraudulent financial statements previously submitted. Most thick account books do not burn readily, and if they are left open to expedite their consumption by fire, the open page is often that part of the book containing the incriminating and fraudulent entries.

Any change in insurance coverage made prior to the fire should be determined. Strange as it may seem, most such changes made by convicted arsonists are made to a smaller coverage in order to divert suspicion. The investigator should therefore be alert to any change.

Analysis of ashes can play a very important part in determining the cause of a fire. Microscopic and laboratory tests of the ash debris may indicate the use of inflammable material not ordinarily used upon the burned premises. The premises should be carefully examined to ascertain if the fire broke out in more than one place simultaneously and if there were more than one independent fire. These manifestations often point to arson.

The ashes may also show the contents of the building in the event it is suspected a claim is being made for articles not believed to have been consumed by fire. The ashes may contain certain residues of wax, paraffin, wicks, oil, fuses, rag, and paper streamers or other material foreign to the premises as judged by the furnishings or the type of business.

Smoke is a complex gaseous mixture carrying more or less solids of varying composition known as soot, and a large quantity of carbon monoxide, and it is the result of imperfect or incomplete combustion or oxidation. Smoke colors may indicate the basic substance being consumed. For example, white smoke is caused by burning hay or other vegetable compounds. Phosphoros also gives off white smoke. Yellow smoke is produced by films and other products having a nitrocellulose base. Black smoke comes from burning oil or other products having a petroleum base. Rubber also gives off black smoke when burned. Notations should always be made of the color of the smoke to determine if the objects allegedly on the premises could have given off the color of smoke produced by the burning.

An arsonist will sometimes seek to produce much smoke by setting a small fire with smoke-producing substances in an isolated area. Certain materials are extremely susceptible to smoke, and insurance may be collected on smoke damage even if the fire does not spread.

Unusual black smoke marks and badly charred surfaces may indicate a petroleum product as the burning agent. Poured on a floor, petroleum burns in the pattern of the pool thus made and sometimes penetrates to cracks in the floor to burn the ceiling below.

All suspicious items of evidence at a fire of dubious origin should be preserved. Some of the items to look for are partly burned streamers strung from one area to another, candle segments, tallow, wax, paraffin, containers of combustibles, and concentrations of inflammable substances foreign to the objects natural to the premises.

When it is sought to attribute a fire of suspicious origin to lightning, it should be ascertained if there was an electrical storm at the approximate time of the fire. A thorough search for melted metal should be made in such a case because this is almost always discoverable after lightning strikes.

Many arsonists claim a short circuit in the electrical system as the cause of a fire. This is seldom true, however, if the fuses are in working order. Expert examination by an electrical specialist should be made in such cases, and the point can be proved or disproved readily.

The investigator must conduct the investigation in a suspected arson case at the earliest possible time following the fire. Doors and windows should be checked to determine if they were locked when the fire occurred. Firemen should be interrogated, and neighbors should be interviewed for information. If it is determined the premises were locked at the time of the fire, the presence of oil-soaked rags or other inflammables takes on added significance.

When the use of oils and chemicals is suspected, samples of the soot or unburned wood should be taken by the investigator for future expert analysis. The newly discovered dye Rhodokrit is being employed with increasing frequency at scenes of fires of dubious origin. The suspected area is powdered with Rhodokrit and allowed to remain twelve hours undisturbed. If the wood contains any traces of kerosene, oil, gasoline, or other fat-dissolving material, the wood will turn red.

In any criminal investigation when the violator is not apprehended at the scene of the crime, it becomes necessary to reconstruct the scene by working backward. This holds true especially in suspected arson cases, which are based almost exclusively on circumstantial evidence.

ARSON INVOLVING VEHICLES

The automotive vehicle, because of its mobility and its fluctuating value and because of the opportunity it offers its owner to execute a mortgage greater than its actual value, lends itself as a particularly suitable instrument to dishonest persons seeking to attain a profit through the wilfull destruction of insured property by burning. In normal times, 90 per cent of all fraudulent arson claims are predicated on the criminal burning of insured automotive vehicles.

An automobile is not generally considered an inflammable object. The modern automobile contains very few inflammable parts. It is constructed of metal motor, chassis, body, and floor, supported by steel braces. In fact the only parts of an automobile that will ordinarily burn are the tires, upholstery, and wiring. Insurance company laboratories have conducted experiments from time to time which have proved that a short circuit may burn the wiring to such a degree as to render it unserviceable, but the blaze will usually burn itself out without setting fire to other parts of the vehicle.

Motivations in automobile arson cases are multifarious and varied. Reasons may be dissatisfaction with the car because of mechanical difficulties, unusual depreciation due to hard use, or lack of need for the vehicle. Financial difficulties based on reduction of income, increased expenses, finance company demands, avoidance of judgment, and sudden pressing gambling debts may supply another series of motives. The third group of prevailing motives is based on domestic difficulties. One spouse may burn the car in which the other spouse philanders. Impending matrimonial difficulties demanding ready cash and the craving to get away may also supply an arson motive.

The investigator should delve into the owner's personal history to ascertain motives, and he should inspect the salvage to determine the previous performance of the car if possible, before interrogating the assured or witnesses. The investigator should interview the finance company, the insurance broker, and the automobile dealer, all of whom may supply sufficient background information to spell out the motive.

214 The Art of Detection

Certain facts or a combination of them, are almost always present in the case of a fire which is natural in origin. Some of these facts are the presence of witnesses at the fire's inception, the destruction of valuable uninsured personal property, the exposure to undue hazard of the assured or members of his family, loss of policy or lack of knowledge that coverage existed, fire breaking out on a busy highway or near a fire station or under circumstances which would indicate rapid extinguishment, an uninsured building such as a garage burning with the vehicle, and actual efforts made by the assured to extinguish the blaze and minimize damage.

Circumstances which may indicate that the fire is of incendiary origin are: wrecking of the car without collision insurance, unsuccessful efforts to trade or sell the vehicle, threatened repossession due to default in time payments, chronic mechanical trouble, policy about to lapse or recently taken out, history of past fires and suspicious claims, prior suspicious liaisons of the assured and the driver of the car, refusal to accept repairs or replacements, and any combination of suspicious or untoward circumstances such as the presence of the assured or the driver on a dark, little traveled road without a satisfactory explanation at the time of the occurrence of the fire.

When the assured is interrogated, the complete history of the vehicle's purchase and its financial status should be obtained. A statement covering the physical condition of the vehicle, the mileage, defects, and equipment may also tend to help to round out the picture of the motive.

The investigator should obtain from the assured complete details covering every incident attendant to the burning of the car. If the imagination of the assured is too vivid, he may describe facts and occurrences which are not ordinarily physically possible. For instance, a stock story is to the effect that the first knowledge the assured had of the fire was when a blaze was seen flashing through the floor boards. This statement is generally not true because floor mats are made of jute and rubber and will burn very slowly, and then only under the application of intense, direct heat.

Numerous experiments have shown that it is difficult to ignite a car so that it will result in a total loss. This fact is understandable when it is known that the only parts susceptible to fire are the tires, wiring, and upholstery, in addition to the fuel. If a cargo of inflammables is carried and they caused the destruction of the vehicle, the investigator should direct special inquiry into the custom, practice, and necessity of transporting such inflammable material.

The investigator should always make a careful inspection of the burned vehicle, which is the salvage and corpus delicti of the case. The salvage should be inspected for the recent removal of any customary extra equipment such as radios, spare tires, heaters, airhorns, fog lights, windshield wipers, and tools. If the car is apparently new, the presence of old, well-worn tires might be an indication that the newer and better tires had been removed prior to the fire. The tool kit should always be inspected to see if the usual tools are missing.

The investigator should ascertain if the gasoline tank cap is in place. Many fires are started by gasoline being siphoned from the tank and frequently, in the hurry and excitement of the occasion, the arsonist will forget to replace the cap.

An expert mechanic should check the gas tank, fuel pump, gas line, electrical system, motor, radiator, and other parts of the vehicle. Special care should be taken to observe heat blisters which are not resultant from the normal progress of the fire, but which may have been caused by gasoline dropped or splashed on the vehicle. If fire allegedly came from the underside of the car, the investigator should examine the area under the floor boards, fenders, and running boards for evidences of flame.

The ground adjacent to the scene of the fire should be searched for a container which may have been used to pour the inflammable fluid on the car. All numbers and other identifying data on the burned vehicle should be checked to ascertain if they coincide with the numbers on the policy.

INVESTIGATION AND SETTLEMENT OF CLAIMS

It is not the purpose of this book to give the investigator the knowledge necessary to adjudicate properly a specialized insurance matter. Rather it is desired to aid the investigator in this or any other activity by suggesting specific methods to obtain the information essential to his current needs. If the investigator is familiar with the background of his work—as he should be—and knows what data are needed to determine a particular moot point, this book is designed to enable him to obtain that required information more expeditiously.

Casualty insurance is a general term applied to various forms of insurance which cover loss or liability resulting principally from accidents, workmen's compensation, plate glass insurance, burglary, employer's liability insurance, automobile liability insurance, theft, boiler and machinery insurance, and personal liability insurance. Limitation is not restricted to this listing, and almost any type of miscellaneous coverage may be added. Losses covered by marine and fire insurance and by law and custom constitute a particular category.

Liability insurance is that type of coverage which protects the assured against loss on account of the liability imposed upon him by law for bodily injury and death accidentally caused to persons—not generally his employees—and for damage to the property of others. It is, briefly, a form of insurance protecting the assured against personal injury or property damage claims of other persons.

Liability insurance embraces automobile liability, contractor's liability, manufacturers' liability, landlord and tenant liability, elevator liability, products liability, professional liability, teams liability, contractual liability, and sports liability.

Fidelity, probate, fiduciary, depositor's forgery, and surety bonds present a divergent sphere of insurance activity. Health, accident, and life insurance present still other gigantic phases of insurance warranting intense specialized investigation directed to the innate problems presented by the ramifications of the several fields.

In the present complex civilization, it is the rare person indeed who is not the possessor or subject of some form of insurance coverage. It is an extremely unique case if a person lives his allotted time without having been subjected to some manner of insurance investigation during his lifetime.

The insurance investigator should bear one cardinal principle in mind always. A claimant in any case should be treated with courtesy, justice, honesty, and equity; and the investigator should remember that no insurance company proposes to take advantage of a claimant with a just claim.

When the witness interviewed is the client of or assured in the investigator's organization, he should be thoroughly questioned on all pertinent details. This will serve as a basis for future investigation, and a sufficiently vigorous line of interrogation will often elicit information which the assured may have been embarrassed or reluctant to submit for fear of prejudicing his case.

The questions propounded should be similar to the ones the witness would have to undergo on cross-examination. The information thus obtained will be of greater value at this point, even if injurious, because a defense and explanation may be prepared. If the same damaging data is elicited at the trial, it may often be too late to do anything toward rectification. It is wise to know the unfavorable aspects of the case in advance rather than to be surprised at a trial.

The witness should be prepared for certain often-repeated pitfalls laid for him by opposing counsel. One of the commonest traps is to ask a question, on cross-examination, in such a manner as to invite a negative and untrue answer. The most prevalent use of this ruse is to ask the witness if he has talked to anyone about the case before testifying. In many instances the witness replies that he has not, even though he has discussed the case many times with the investigator. The reason for the misstatement is the witness's belief that it would be prejudicial to his case if it were known that he discussed it before trial. After proving that the witness did, in fact, discuss the case, the cross-examining attorney will emphasize that the witness is unworthy of belief. This rather common trap should be explained by the investigator, and the witness, thus forewarned, should not fall into it.

In lawsuits defended by insurance companies, the only persons or parties appearing as litigants of record are the claimant and the defendant. As far as the jury knows or is concerned, no insurance company is involved. Because of the likelihood of sympathy for the plaintiff if it is known to the jury that an insurance company, instead of the defendant, will pay the verdict, most jurisdictions bar a claimant from showing that an insurance company is conducting the defense.

Sharp practitioners for plaintiffs often seek to circumvent this prohibition by soliciting a reference to the insurance company, especially asking the witnesses questions pertaining to the time and the place when the investigator took the statement in an effort to connect the insurance company with the case. When an attorney comes into the picture he, and not the insurance company, actually represents the defendant. Therefore the investigator should alert all of his witnesses to the pitfall, and they should be admonished to speak of the attorney and not of the insurance company which retained him.

The good investigator should keep in mind that the success

of any interrogation often depends on where it takes place. The presence of relatives or co-workers may, in certain instances, prevent the witness from speaking openly. In certain other instances such moral support to the witness may be advantageous. All of the elements and aspects of the case should be evaluated by the investigator when he chooses the place of interview; and the time, place, and circumstances of conducting the interrogation should be picked with the ultimate thought in mind of obtaining the most complete information with the fewest possible hindrances.

All claimants should be checked with the records kept by clearing houses for the benefit of insurance companies. This service will appraise the investigator if the claimant is a "repeater" or "flopper." Frequently the time element may compel an immediate search of a claimant's background, in which event court records, police blotters, and state motor vehicle files will prove of inestimable aid in obtaining some background of the current plaintiff. Even if the subject is not a professional "repeater," the record of prior accidents is invaluable in determining if the injuries presently claimed had been sustained in a prior accident.

Certain background information should be obtained in every case. The coverage, according to the nature of the insurance, should be verified first. Sometimes a particular type of claim reported by the assured or his broker does not come within the exact purview of the policy. Payment in such instances would be in error. The investigator should obtain immediately the following basic data: age, residence address, business address, occupation and earnings of the injured person; racial origin; character; position in community; reputation; marital status in detail; medical expenses; nature and extent of personal injuries, ascertaining if the injuries are such as to have been caused by the accident in question or from a previous accident; prior medical and accident history; and prior history of usage of alcohol or drugs. In inquiring into the medical history of the injured person, the investigator should ascertain specifically if the person has diabetes and uses insulin, because accidents resulting from insulin shock are increasing in number. The investigator should obtain the foregoing data in addition to the complete story of the accident as related by the witness in his own words. Supplemental and additional information may be procured from insurance clearing house reports, police blotter reports, motor vehicle bureau reports, photographs, traffic accident reports, hospital records, doctors' records, physical examination, and statements of other witnesses. The information should be obtained pursuant to the practice and requirements existing in the respective jurisdictions.

It is axiomatic that law is based on common sense. It is the facts, however, which are frequently so distorted and confused as to cause the misapplication of an unrelated theory of law, resulting in a miscarriage of justice. In personal injury cases, claimants may change facts for their personal gain, and witnesses may be motivated by sympathy or friendship to avoid the truth. The claims investigator must exercise every iota of his native ingenuity and common sense to separate the evidentiary wheat from the chaff, and to keep it so separated until the time of trial.

The investigator will often be called upon to interpret the dramatic quality of a case. There are non-evidentiary factors that often guide and sway the final conclusion in a disputed matter. Will the claimant be brought in on a stretcher? Will there be a weeping widow with several children in the courtroom? Will the claimant have a baby in her arms? Will the plaintiff be an attractive young woman who is scarred? Conditions such as these can work havoc with the good intentions of the jurors to predicate their decisions purely on the evidence submitted. An evaluation of the factors *prior* to the trial may uncover potentialities which make it important to endeavor to effect a settlement when no such attempt would have been made ordinarily.

There are other factors related to the dramatic qualities of a case of which an alert investigator should be cognizant. Has the attorney representing the claimant obtained many substantial verdicts in the local courts? What is the local reputation of the attorney? Sometimes the lawyer is the scion of a locally prominent and esteemed family, and regardless of whether he is good, bad, or indifferent, the jury is reluctant to turn down a plea by him. It is the case of "the king can do no wrong" and everything this type of lawyer says will generally be accepted. Other factors to consider are the political and civic stature of the claimant or his lawyer; the prior associations, if any, between any of the counsel and the judge; and the reputation of the defendant. The defendant in a case might be the local villain, and the intense dislike in which he is held by the community might be reflected in the verdict against him in the current case. The jury, of course, is not presumed to know that an insurance company will pay the verdict. The community's regard or disregard for specific racial minorities should also be considered when a member of any such minority group is a party litigant. Due deliberation should be given to any of the foregoing factors if they are found to be present, in an effort to avoid the trial of those cases where it is suspected that the verdict may be influenced by emotion, prejudice, sympathy, influence, or impression.

The investigator in a personal injury case should remember that the claims ordinarily fall into three divisions: lost earning; medical costs; and pain and suffering of the claimant. It is the latter which is so tenuous in the minds of a jury and which cannot be confined to any limitations by formula or rule. It is this single factor which sometimes inspires a jury to exceed its own good judgment when it is motivated by sympathy or prejudice. Paradoxically, it is the latter division which should be mentioned least by the investigator in endeavoring to effect settlement.

In discussing the settlement of a case with a claimant out of court it is usually effective if the claimant writes on a piece of paper the time he has lost from work and the amount of wages lost based on daily, weekly, or monthly remuneration. He should write down also the amount of money spent for medical attention, and the figures should be totaled. The visual presentation of claimant's actual loss frequently will reduce exaggerated ideas of the damages sustained. The fact that the claimant himself writes the figures often tends to instill a belief that he is telling the investigator what to do, and the receipt of the amount as set forth by the claimant in writing strengthens his belief that he is winning a victory. Another important element when such a procedure is employed is the fact that if a settlement is not effected, the investigator has a record in the claimant's handwriting showing the exact amount, and this will serve as a bar to a swollen figure that might be submitted at a trial. The investigator, as a practical matter, will generally offer a sum in settlement exceeding the amount of actual expenditures, the excess being the equitable remuneration for pain and suffering, although this factor is not discussed in the actual negotiations.

Every case should be settled for what it is reasonably worth and not for what the claimant demands. The disparity between the amount asked and the amount offered may be astounding, but very frequently the plaintiff will be given food for thought by submitting an exceedingly low offer to him. During the course of negotiating a case for settlement, the investigator should keep his senses alerted for any material fact disclosed that may be used at a future trial if the settlement negotiations fail. The investigator should be general in his remarks insofar as he possibly can, and he should let his adversary do the bulk of the talking. No anxiety should be shown in an effort to settle a case, while at the same time the investigator should not be guilty of laches by not settling a serious injury case.

All cases involving serious injuries should be handled expeditiously, and when the defendant is clearly liable, immediate settlement should be made, the amounts paid being based on serious injury, moderate injury, slight injury, and in some instances no injury. In cases when the liability is questionable, prompt consideration of settlement should be made, but when no legal liability exists, the investigator ordinarily should make no effort to settle.

There should be no precipitation in increasing the offer of settlement. The increase should be brought up gradually, and the claimant should be made to wait short intervals before the offer is increased. Often when dealing directly with a claimant, before he has retained an attorney, the investigator may use the powerful argument that the full amount offered currently will go to the claimant, instead of being paid out partially in attorney's fees.

Letters used by the investigator are important factors in the transaction of routine business. A communication should not be phrased or worded carelessly. It should be brief, concise, and interesting enough to hold the attention of the reader, and it must submit argument or proof of the importance of the request made or the proposition advanced. The letter must be persuasive and inducive, and, whenever possible, it should end in a "clincher" or emphatic line which suggests the impossibility or foolishness of any action contrary to that outlined in the proposal of the communication.

The investigator should retain the communications of all persons who file claims and of those interested persons who answer correspondence relative to claims. There may be a possibility of using these documents to develop a future prosecution growing out of the use of the mails to defraud.

Accidents occurring the day before the expiration date of the policy, or on the expiration date, should be subjects for careful scrutiny against the possibility of collusion.

Quantitatively the property damage cases are the bane of the existence of the insurance investigator. It is a matter of common knowledge that much collusion exists in this kind of insurance. Frequently the drivers of two automobiles involved in an accident will foist the onus of their negligence to an insurance company in small claims. Often they are guilty of contributory negligence. Still more frequently, unscrupulous mechanics and garages will amplify costs of repairs and pad the bills. Nevertheless, the investigator should not delay in making a prompt settlement in a property damage case when it appears that in doing so the possible birth of a personal injury claim is prevented.

No matter how serious a property damage case is, the investigator will always know what the "roof" or limit of liability may be. The financial damage must fall within certain defined monetary limits, and no more ever need be paid beyond those limits. In personal injury claims, however, regardless of how slight the injury apparently is, there is no assurance that the claim will not grow into gigantic proportions because of complications and disabilities proximately resulting from the basic injury.

The insurance investigator will probably deal with the same attorneys again and again in his territory, and he should never gloat or glory in any victory over them. Nor should he ever boast that he has bested an attorney in a settlement. Such actions will serve to put the attorney on his mettle and foster a determination to be cautious if he ever negotiates with the same investigator on another matter.

Immediately after the investigation, decision is generally made whether the case is one for settlement or one for trial. The timing of settlement talks is important, and should be given full concentration by the investigator. It is dependent upon all the facts and circumstances in the case. Sometimes it may not be advisable to discuss settlement immediately after the death of a near relative, or too soon after a very serious injury. These angles must be considered in the handling of the individual case.

It is sometimes difficult to determine if a person is a minor. For this reason, in order to guard against conducting negotiations with a suspected minor, the investigator should ascertain the age of the subject from an indisputable source. If there is any element of doubt, a minor's guardian should be appointed, and he should function in conformity with the laws of the jurisdiction.

Insurance companies are almost universally obliged by statute to set aside a certain amount of money as a reserve in each lawsuit to back up and assure payment on the contingent liability arising out of the possible judgments to be rendered against their assureds. The investigator will be called upon to determine the approximate liability of a claim, even before settlement is discussed, so that the proper reserve may be set up. There is no true denominator or formula the investigator may use which will satisfy the state examining authorities as to the correctness of the reserve. The investigator's experience, acumen, and ordinary common sense should guide him. What might be a suitable reserve of one thousand dollars in the case of a scrubwoman who broke her leg, might be, and should be, increased to ten or twenty-five thousand dollars in the case of a dancer with a similar injury.

The average insurance company will continually exert pressure on its investigators to settle cases in order to reduce the reserves set up. These drives generally take place the latter part of the year. The procedure is known to most attorneys who are active in the practice of the so-called negligence cases. The astute investigator can generally turn this practice to the advantage of the insurance company. A call to the claimant's attorney toward the end of the year, with the view of discussing settlement and at the same time conveying the inference that it is desired to eliminate the reserve on the particular case, often presents a graceful opening to the investigator if he is not prone to show his anxiety to effect settlement. Even when the investigator is not under pressure to settle the case, he may sometimes effect a satisfactory settlement with this approach, because the attorney may believe the offer to be an inflated one based on the desire to eliminate the reserve.

Fidelity claims do not present the same need for speed as do casualty claims. The groundwork for final settlement is generally laid on the first visit to the obligee's office. Prior to the visit the investigator should check the central index files of the clearing house serving his particular company in order to determine if the assured or the defaulter were ever turned down on prior bonds. A complete résumé should be obtained from the records.

The investigator should examine the bond to determine exact coverage, and he should begin to lay the foundation in general terms for the final elimination of all questionable items. A fully executed proof of loss and an audit by a reputable firm will aid the investigator to ascertain the regularity of the claim. Because of the greater length of time necessarily spent in investigating fidelity cases, the investigator may often be subjected to criticism. To offset this, it is of great help to capitalize upon those cases where quick settlements are made. This capitalization is in effect the propagandizing of the quickly settled case by disseminating that information widely in order to show that a delay in a current fidelity case is not capricious but due to the need for a thorough investigation.

Delay in a fidelity investigation will often precipitate an offer to accept a lesser amount than originally claimed. It is not for the purpose of beating down an honest claimant, however, that a delay is advantageous in this type of investigation. All too often when there is an actual defalcation or embezzlement, especially when the culprit is not immediately apprehended, the assured will claim that a much greater amount was stolen than was actually the case.

The fidelity investigation should cover, in addition to the general history of the case, all data pertaining to any previous shortage in the principal's accounts, definite information relative to each item claimed, the date of loss of each item, the date of first discovery by the obligee, the history of principal's employment, and his financial condition. The latter is important in efforts to obtain recoverable assets in the way of salvage.

Considerable preparation must be made by the investigator in fidelity claim investigations, primarily because most of the facts are in the possession of the obligee. The hazard of a fidelity risk is as much dependent upon the character of the obligee as upon that of the principal. Too many obligees use the excuse of an admitted loss to recoup losses which are not the result of dishonesty on the part of an identifiable employee but are due to inventory shortage. The investigator should accept no items unless there is convincing proof that they were lost through the misconduct of an identifiable principal.

Frequently cases arise which indicate that after discovery of a defalcation by the obligee, the defaulter has been allowed to make good his shortage, and has been retained in the obligee's employ, with no report made to the insurance company. Later, when another shortage develops, the obligee reports it, this time as a claim. The withholding of facts of the prior shortage generally bars recovery on the current claim, even if the obligee may have acted in apparent good faith on the previous occasion, being motivated by sympathy or for some other reason. In such a case, the investigator should obtain the date of the first dishonest act because frequently subsequent entries are made in records, and transactions entered into, which are occasioned by efforts to cover the original act. The application for the bond originally executed by the assured should be carefully scrutinized for possible misrepresentations.

In fidelity insurance the principal defaulter stands between the insurance company and the person suffering the loss. The importance of ascertaining the financial status of the embezzler or defaulter cannot be too strongly emphasized because at all times it is he who is primarily liable to the person suffering the loss.

In fidelity claims, as in burglary and theft claims, there is not the harmony of interest between the company and its assured as exists in those types of insurance where the insurance company pays its claims against the assured directly to a third party. In the latter cases the interests of the insured and the company are harmonious in resisting mutually and jointly the claims of a common adversary.

In fidelity claims, the theory of indemnity for liability to others is lacking. This type of policy contemplates making good to the assured the loss which he himself suffers by reason of the theft of his personal property, pursuant to certain definements. Thus in fidelity claims it is not a third person but the assured himself who becomes the claimant. It is wise for the investigator to keep this distinction in mind always, because the claimant in the fidelity case may not be a person upon whom reliance may be placed as implicitly as it may upon the assured whose aid he solicits in combating the disputed claim of a third-party claimant. The self-interest which motivates the claimant in the fidelity case is sometimes as larcenous as that of the defaulter.

The investigator should always obtain police blotter reports in fidelity, theft, or burglary losses, and particular notice should be taken of the time the crime was reported to the police and the loss as stated at that time. Prior losses and coverage in other companies, should also be checked.

If it is suspected that a burglary may be fabricated or the worth of the contents allegedly stolen has been exaggerated, vouchers or papers attesting to, describing, or indicating the character of the articles stolen should be obtained. The place of purchase and the name of the purchaser should also be procured. A full list of all members of the assured's household, including domestics and other help having access to the premises, may be of assistance. In suspicious cases, a discreet financial check-up of the assured's affairs should be made, particularly to ascertain if recent mortgages were taken on the stolen articles. The absence of damage to household or business property, such as doors, windows, drawers, files, or desks after a burglary should also be noted when personal articles were stolen from the premises.

In Workmen's Compensation cases, investigation of the claim is directed to the nature of the accident and the extent of the injury, together with the resulting disability, as well as to the question of whether the occurrence was such as might arise out of and in the course of the injured person's employment.

The investigator should obtain wage statements, because companies obtain premiums on the amount actually paid in wages, and if a man has been working only two or three days a week, it would be unfair to the company to pay him on the basis of a full week's compensation. Laws on this point, however, are at variance in different states. When business is below par, and layoffs are imminent, statistics show an abnormal accident rate and longer time of incapacitation. Protective clearing house information is also available on professional fakers in this field.

In cases of suspected faking, many of the shadowing suggestions contained elsewhere in this book may be employed to ascertain if the claimant is active in sports or other physical activities. Moving pictures are frequently taken of claimants who declare physical incapacity, showing them actively engaged in playing baseball, football, tennis, or other game. The native ingenuity of the investigator must serve him in this field also, and his efforts should respond to the exigencies of the situation. One investigator "broke" the case of a suspected medical faker by tailing him to a movie. While the suspected faker was in the movie, the air was let out of a tire on his automobile. When the claimant, who was supposed to be totally incapacitated, came out of the theater and saw the flat tire, he did not call a service station. Instead, he changed the tire himself, apparently with ease, and drove away. Pictures taken of this occurrence later resulted in the questionable case being thrown out of court.

In the average compensation case, the investigator should ascertain the following:

1. Coverage, including name and address of assured, nature of business, place and time of accident.
2. Description of accident; statements of injured person and eyewitnesses.
3. Whether the accident occurred in the course of employment.
4. Whether the injured person was guilty of wilful misconduct, such as being intoxicated, indulging in horseplay or practical jokes, violating a law or express rules; or whether the injuries were deliberately self-inflicted as in an attempt at suicide.

5. Details of employment like compensation.
6. Whether the injuries of the employee were due to the negligence of a third person.
7. Description of injuries; medical expenses.
8. A check on prior accidents of the injured person and a consideration of any other factors which might indicate malingering, feigning, or aggravating injuries.
9. If the employee died as a result of the accident, a complete investigation should be made to determine whether he lived with or supported a wife, the names and ages of any children, and the names, addresses, and ages of all dependents.

Inquisitiveness, imagination, and initiative should be a part of every insurance investigator's activity. He should exercise these traits liberally in every phase of his work. The investigator's storehouse of experience should be constantly called upon, and at the same time it should be replenished continually. Simple, obvious solutions will frequently result from the application of methods developed by a little thought and foresight.

A classic example of the application of determination and initiative by an investigator to unravel a bothersome mystery is illustrated in the case of a happily married woman who left a suicide note and some clothes on a high bridge, apparently before jumping into the swiftly flowing river beneath. The distraught husband could advance no reason for suicide. The couple had worked in the same government office and had been married for several years. The husband knew nothing about his wife's family except that they lived somewhere in the South. Some time later, the husband entered the claim for the insurance on his wife's life, although her body was not recovered from the river nor had it been found elsewhere.

The insurance investigator assigned to the case found nothing in the preliminary investigation to indicate fraud or collusion. Nevertheless he was dissatisfied with the seeming mystery surrounding the wife's background, and he decided to make an attempt to unravel this unknown factor.

The investigator examined the application for marriage license executed by the wife and husband prior to their marriage. On this application, signed by the bride, were the names of her parents and her place of birth. The parents were listed as dead. The investigator wrote to the postmaster of a little town in Alabama listed by the bride as her birthplace, inquiring if any persons lived in the town under the surname of the wife before her marriage.

The reply from the postmaster stated that a colored family by that named lived in the community, and he gave the first names of the couple he referred to. These names coincided with the names of the parents given on the marriage application who were listed as dead.

The investigator, sensing a "hot" clue, proceeded to the town in question and immediately went to the home of the couple named by the postmaster. He found a pleasant, elderly colored couple whose daughter and grandchild lived with them. The daughter was an olive-skinned, attractive girl, and the child was a fawn-colored baby. To the pleasure and surprise of the investigator, the daughter immediately admitted that she was the missing wife who was believed to have committed suicide. She tearfully stated that she never told her husband she had colored blood, and when she found herself pregnant, she was frantic that the baby would betray her secret. She explained she thought the easiest way to leave her husband was by the means of simulated suicide. The element of insurance never entered her mind, she told the investigator, and she did not know her husband had applied for the proceeds of the policy taken out on her life.

This tragic story emphasizes the futility of blindly and mechanically following specific directions, or conventional facilities, in handling insurance settlements. Knowledge and learning are insufficient if no common sense, judgment, and wisdom are employed. Knowledge can become a useless and ornamental appendage without the ability to apply it to a practical purpose. Wisdom is the practical application of knowledge, and the efficient investigator will apply his theoretical knowledge of investigation toward the exercise of good judgment.

CHAPTER THIRTEEN

THE NEED OF RESOURCE-FULNESS

A PROPERLY conducted investigation enlists the aid of all sciences, arts, and occupations to the end that the sum total of relevant human knowledge is available for the use of the investigator.

It is the function of an investigator to procure evidentiary data which lighten the darkness of the unknown. The more complete the investigation, the more light is shed and the more answers are supplied to the questions presented.

The investigator must remember that acts of omission can be as effective as acts of commission in affecting the determination of moot issues. Acts of omission, when available information is not obtained or when dubious information received is not verified, manifest themselves in miscarriages of justice and erroneous adjudications.

An incomplete investigation is an erroneous investigation because a conclusion predicated upon inadequate facts is based on quicksand.

No investigator should ever take it upon himself to conclude that any problem is not solvable until every avenue and resource known to the science of investigation is exhausted. More often than not, the answer to the particular riddle will be found if this policy is followed.

When an investigator throws up his hands and admits defeat, the reason for this action does not lie necessarily in his possible laziness and ineptitude. The danger may lurk in the fact that the investigator has made his conclusions after exhausting only those avenues of investigation of which he is aware. He has exercised palpably good faith in his belief that nothing else can be done.

This hazard must be overcome by all investigators if they are to operate at top efficiency. The investigator should be familiar with all of the methods and procedures applicable to his particular field, some of which are set forth in this book. If no suggestion for new or additional action can be found in any of the authorities, the investigator should accept the challenge and strain his mental faculties to the utmost to create his own innovation to cope with a given situation.

Novel investigative methods are developed daily, depending on the exigencies of a particular situation, and no investigator should ever hesitate to set precedents. It is far better in the final analysis to attempt difficult solutions, even if the chances of error are obviously present, than it is to take refuge in the spineless adage "If you don't do anything, you don't do it wrong."

The investigator will find there is no restriction upon the form of a method of procedure employed to attain a specific end. The pattern of any suggestion or plan should be molded to fit the contour of the facts developed by the occasion. Adaptability and elasticity born of originality and imagination should be present in every formulated investigative plan.

In an effort to apprehend violators, the investigator must not confuse the lawful stratagems and ruses available to him with entrapment. It has been pointed out, and it cannot be too strongly emphasized, that while initiative and perseverance are desirable, no unduly zealous investigator should overreach himself by seducing a person into the commission of a crime which he would not have committed ordinarily. The investigator must remember also that no case is important enough to risk his integrity and reputation in the commission of an unauthorized, illegal act, even if it is in the furtherance of a praiseworthy and lawful investigation.

While every investigator should endeavor to proceed according to a clearly defined plan, seeking out evidence he deems germane to the known issues, he should not be prone to dismiss arbitrarily, as valueless, evidence not at the moment directly related to the issues. The true importance of testimony and physical evidence cannot be appreciated fully and evaluated until the ultimate adjudication of the questions of fact adduced. For this reason, the more facts ascertained, and the more evidence obtained, the better the chance of ultimately fitting the disjointed particles of the jigsaw puzzle into a complete, coherent, understandable picture of the scene sought to be completed.

The trained investigator's mind should react like a thirsty sponge in absorbing and retaining all facts developed during the course of an investigation. Later, when the determination must be made, the relevant, important data can be squeezed out of the wealth of retained evidence and sequestered for appropriate action. When an investigation is completed and the facts are compiled, there should be no other sources of evidence bearing on undetermined questions of fact left untapped if the necessary evidence could have been obtained with reasonable effort and diligence.

Difficult cases may present clues indicating a justification of the pursuit of certain specific theories, which is in reality an extension of the trial-and-error system in investigation. If an investigator's common sense and good judgment tell him that an unproductive theory is unsound and should be discarded, he should take the step and submerge his personal pride and obstinacy. The abandonment of a course of action, even if the results are negative, brings the case that much closer to successful solution by eliminating a step which ordinarily would have to be taken in the search for the right answer.

The good investigator must be a practical psychologist, and a study of this subject may help in the handling of people. The greatest aid, however, will come from the investigator's own analysis of each person and situation with which he is confronted.

All the authorities combined do not give a truly effective formula for the procurement of information from reluctant persons. Each case and each problem rests on the specific peculiarities and characteristics inherent in the persons involved. The investigator should realize that every person possesses an affinity, knowledge, or attachment for some subject which is close to his heart. Once the investigator invokes the formula by which the door to this subject is opened, full co-operation may generally be secured.

There is a story about a group of reporters who traveled on the same train with Herbert Hoover when he was en route to receive formal notice of his nomination as president of the United States. All efforts to interview the reticent Mr. Hoover brought a short, succinct "yes" or "no" to the questions propounded, with absolutely no elaboration.

As the train sped through Nevada, a reporter remembered that Mr. Hoover had been an active mining engineer. With this in mind the resourceful reporter commented, "This is still pick-and-shovel mining country."

The engineer in Mr. Hoover rebelled at this misstatement, and he forthwith delivered a long harangue on modern mining methods. With this, the ice was broken, and the expansive Mr. Hoover went on to answer fully the interrogations submitted by the reporters.

Investigation in police work is the instrument whereby life and property are protected, and it acts as a guarantor of the peaceful and secure way of communal life, developed by our modern civilization.

Investigation in the non-criminal field is the insurer of business, commerce, and industry against the risks of cheats, frauds, and connivers. It is the protector of the trusting against charlatans, the barrier against the unscrupulous, and the avenger of the victimized.

The natural result of investigation is truth, upon which the foundation of justice is based. The investigator is a disciple of truth, and his credo, in the language of Robert Herrick, should be,

> "Attempt the end, and never stand to doubt;
> Nothing's so hard but search will find it out."

BIBLIOGRAPHY

Accident Investigation Manual. Northwestern University Traffic Institute (1940).

ALEXANDER, WILLIAM. *Modern Photography with Modern Miniature Cameras.* London (1934).

American Rifleman's Encyclopedia. Peters Cartridge Co., Cincinnati (1902).

AMES, DANIEL T. *Ames on Forgery.* New York (1900).

ANDES, LOUIS EDGAR. *The Treatment of Paper for Special Purposes.* London (1923).

ANDREWS, F. L. *Ashes and Their Meaning.* Florida School for State Fire Marshals, Jacksonville (1945).

ASKINS, CAPTAIN CHARLES, JR. *The Art of Handgun Shooting.* New York (1941).

ASTBURY, W. T. *Fundamentals of Fibre Structure.* London (1933).

AUTENREITH, WILHELM. *Detection of Poisons.* Philadelphia (1928).

BALY, E. C. C. *Spectroscopy.* London (1929).

BATTLEY, HARRY. *Single Fingerprints.* New Haven (1937).

BEAUMONT, ROBERTS. *Standard Cloths.* London (1916).

BECKMAN, THEODORE N. *Credits and Collection in Theory and Practice.* New York (1939).

BELLING, JOHN. *Use of the Microscope.* New York (1930).

BENNET, H. *Commercial Waxes.* New York (1944).

BERTILLON, ALPHONSE. *Identification Anthropometrique* (Anthropometrical Identification). Melun (1885).

BERTILLON, ALPHONSE. *Photographie Judiciaire* (Judicial Photography). Paris (1890).

BIELASKI, BRUCE. *Tying in Corpus Delecti with Suspect.* Florida School for State Fire Marshals, Jacksonville (1945).

BLACKBURN AND CADELL. *Detection of Forgery.* London (1913).

BLAIR, JULIAN M. *Photography.* New York (1945).

BLANCHARD, RALPH H. *Liability and Compensation Insurance.* New York (1917).

BLUMANN, SIGISMUND. *Photographic Workroom Handbook.* San Francisco (1930).

BLUMANN, SIGISMUND. *Photographic Handbook.* San Francisco (1935).

BOND, HORATIO. *Fire Defense.* Boston (1941).

BORCHARD, EDWIN M. *Convicting the Innocent.* New Haven (1932).

BRIDGES, B. C. *Practical Fingerprinting.* New York (1942).

BRODE, WALLACE R. *Chemical Spectroscopy.* New York (1939).

BROMLEY, H. A. *Outline of Stationary Testing.* London (1913).

BROOKES, V. J. AND ALYEA, H. N. *Poisons—Their Properties, Chemical Identification, Symptoms, and Emergency Treatments.* New York (1946).

BULBULIAN, ARTHUR H. *Facial Prosthesis.* Philadelphia (1945).

BURTON, E. F. AND KOHL, W. H. *The Electron Microscope.* New York (1946).

CAHALANE, CORNELIUS F. *The Policeman.* New York (1923).

CALLAN, GEORGE D. AND STEPHENSON, RICHARD. *Police Methods for Today and Tomorrow.* Newark (1939).

CAMPBELL, JOHN D. *Everyday Psychiatry.* Philadelphia (1945).

CARVALHO, DAVID V. *Forty Centuries of Inks.* New York (1904).

CARVALHO AND SPARKES. *Crime in Ink.* New York (1929).

CASSELL, R. J. *Art of Collecting.* New York (1913).

CASTELLANOS, ISRAEL. *Identification Problems, Civil and Criminal.* Brooklyn (1939).

CHAMOT, E. M. AND MASON, C. W. *Handbook of Chemical Microscopy.* New York (1938).

CHANCEY, J. B. *Preservation of Arson Evidence.* Florida School for State Fire Marshals, Jacksonville (1945).

CHAPEL, CHARLES EDWARD. *Fingerprinting.* New York (1941).

COCHRAN, WILLIAM B. *Law Lexicon.* Cincinnati (1924).

CONWELL, CHIC. *The Professional Thief.* Annotated and Interpreted by Edwin H. Sutherland. Chicago (1937).

COOPER, F. J. *Textile Chemistry.* London (1923).

CORNELIUS, ASHER L. *Cross-Examination of Witnesses.* Indianapolis (1929).

CORRINGTON, JULIAN D. *Working with the Microscope.* New York (1941).

COWAN, T. W. *Waxcraft.* London (1908).

COWDRY, E. V. *Microscopic Technique in Biology and Medicine.* Baltimore (1943).

DESCHIN, JACOB. *Making Pictures with a Miniature Camera.* New York (1937).

DE SOLA, RALPH. *Microfilming.* New York (1944).

DILNOT, GEORGE. *Great Detectives and Their Methods.* New York (1928).

EAMES AND DANIELS. *An Introduction to Plant Anatomy.* New York (1925).

EBERSOLE, J. FRANKLIN. *Bank Management.* New York (1940).

ELSE AND GARROW. *Detection of Crime Dealing with the Technique of Microscopy and Examination of Dust.* London (1934).

FERRI, ENRICO. *Criminal Sociology.* Edited by William W. Smithers. Boston (1917).

FLOHERTY, JOHN J. *Inside the F.B.I.* Philadelphia (1943).

FOX, J. J. AND BOWLES, T. H. *The Analysis of Pigments, Paints, and Varnishes.* London (1927).

FRAZER, PERSIFOR. *Bibliotics or Study of Documents.* Philadelphia (1901).

FRESNIUS, T. W. *Introduction to Qualitative Chemical Analysis.* London (1921).

FRICKE, CHARLES W. *Criminal Investigation.* Los Angeles (1933).

GAGE, SIMON HENRY. *The Microscope.* Ithaca (1941).

GARDNER, HENRY A. *Physical and Chemical Examination of Paints, Varnishes, Lacquers, and Colors.* Washington (1933).

GARRETT, ANNETTE. *Interviewing, It's Principles and Methods.* New York (1942).

GEYER, ANDREW. *Registry of Water Marks and Trade Marks.* New York (1906).

GIBB, THOMAS R. P. *Optical Methods of Chemical Analysis.* New York (1942).

GILLIN, JOHN LEWIS. *Criminology and Penology.* New York (1945).

GONZALES, T. A. *Legal Medicine and Toxicology.* New York (1940).

GROSS, HANS. *Criminal Psychology.* Boston (1918).

GROSS, HANS. *Criminal Investigation.* London (1934).

GUNTHER, CHARLES O. AND GUNTHER, J. D. *Identification of Firearms.* New York (1935).

HARDING, T. S. *Popular Practice of Fraud.* New York (1935).

HATCHER, JULIAN S. *Textbook of Firearms Investigation.* Plantersville (1934).

HAYNES, FRED E. *Criminology.* New York (1935).

HEALY, WILLIAM AND HEALY, MARY. *Pathological Lying, Accusation, and Swindling.* Boston (1926).

HIND AND RANDLES. *Handbook of Photomicrography.* New York (1927).

HOLLOWAY, HARRY D. *The Science of Fingerprint Classification.* Columbus (1941).

HOWE, JAMES V. *The Modern Gunsmith,* New York (1934).

HUNTER, DARD. *Paper Making Through Eighteen Centuries.* New York (1930).

"Identification of Shells," *Journal of Criminal Law and Criminology,* Vol. 23, No. 3, Chicago, 1932. Translated from *Revue Internationale de Criminalistique,* Vol. 4, No. 5.

Identification Systems and Equipment. Remington Rand Co. Buffalo (1937).

IRONS, WATROUS H. *Commercial Credit and Collection Practice.* New York (1913).

JAHANS, GORDON A. *Paper Testing and Chemistry for Printers.* Bath (1931).

JONES, FLOYD L. *Valid or Forged.* New York (1938).

KENLON, JOHN. *Fires and Fire Fighters.* New York (1913).

KINSLEY, W. J. *Typewriter Identification.* New York (1911).

KNIFFIN, H. R. *Masks.* Peoria (1931).

KNIFFIN, WILLIAM H. *Better Banking.* New York (1934).

KREML, FRANKLIN M. *The Evidence Handbook for Police.* Edited by David Geeting Monroe, Northwestern University Traffic Institute (1943).

LEE, BOLLES. *Microtomist's Vade-Mecum.* Edited by J. V. Gatenby and E. V. Cowdry. Philadelphia (1928).

LEHNER, SIGMUND. *Ink Manufacture.* London (1926).

LENZ, ALFRED DAVID. *The Alfred David Lenz System of Lost Wax Casting.* New York (1933).

LUCAS, A. *Forensic Chemistry and Scientific Criminal Investigation.* New York (1935).

MAGEE, JOHN H. *General Insurance.* Chicago (1942).

MALTZ, MAXWELL. *Evolution of Plastic Surgery.* New York (1946).

Manual for Courts Martial. U. S. Government Printing Office, War Department Document 14-a (1928).

Manual for Instruction. New York Fire Department. Edited by Lowell M. Limpus. New York (1940).

MARES, G. C. *The History of the Typewriter.* London (1909).

MATTHEWS, J. M. *The Textile Fibres.* New York (1913).

MAY, LUKE S. "The Identification of Knives, Tools, and Instruments, a Positive Science," *American Journal of Police Science,* Vol. 1, No. 3 (1930).

MEES, CHARLES E. *Fundamentals of Photography.* Rochester (1938).

MILES, W. G. *Pyromania.* Florida School for State Fire Marshals, Jacksonville (1945).

MILLAR, WILLIAM. *Plastering, Plain and Decorative.* Edinburgh (1927).

Minimizing Losses Through Employee Dishonesty. U. S. Fidelity and Guarantee Company. Baltimore (1943).

MITCHELL, C. A. *Documents and Their Scientific Examination.* London (1922).

MITCHELL, C. A. "Estimated Age of Inks in Writing," *Analyst* (1920).

MITCHELL, C. A. *The Scientific Detective and the Expert Witness.* New York (1931).

MITCHELL AND HEPWORTH. *Inks—Their Composition and Manufacture.* London (1922).

MOTT-SMITH, LORENZO. *Financial Problems of Installment Selling.* New York (1931).

MURCHISON, CARL. *Criminal Intelligence.* Worcester (1926).

OLYANOVA, MADYA. *What Does Your Handwriting Reveal?* New York (1929).

OSBORNE, ARTHUR S. "Proof of Handwriting," *Illinois Law Review* (1911).

OSBORNE, ARTHUR S. Questioned Documents. New York (1929).

Penal Law and Code of Criminal Procedure of the State of New York. Annotated by John T. Cook. Albany (1917).

PERKINS, ROLLIN M. Elements of Police Science. Chicago (1942).

Photomicrography. Eastman Kodak Co. Rochester (1932).

PRENDERGAST AND STEINER. Credit and Its Uses. New York (1931).

PURDEY, J. A. AND PURDEY, T. D. S. The Shotgun. New York (1937).

PURVIS, MELVIN. American Agent. Garden City (1936).

Questions and Answers for Examination in Casualty Insurance Given to Applicants for State Agent's Licenses. Hartford (1946).

RADLEY, J. A., AND GRANT, JULIUS. Fluorescence and Analysis in Ultraviolet Light. New York (1939).

REXFORD, JOHN. What Handwriting Indicates. New York (1904).

RHODES, HENRY T. F. The Craft of Forgery. London (1937).

Richards on the Law of Insurance. Edited by Rowland H. Long. New York (1932).

RICHARDSON, WILLIAM P. Law of Evidence. Brooklyn (1928).

ROBINSON, HENRY MORTON. Science Catches the Criminal. Indianapolis (1935).

SCHIRESON, HENRY J. As Others See You: The Story of Plastic Surgery. New York (1938).

SCHWARTZ, LOUIS E. Trial of Automobile Accident Cases. Albany (1928).

"Scientific Identification of Firearms and Bullets," Journal of Criminal Law and Criminology, Vol. 17-2 (1926).

Scientific Laboratory Services of the State Bureau of Identification, New Jersey State Police. Trenton (1946).

SCOTT, CHARLES C. Photographic Evidence. Kansas City (1942).

SHILLABER, CHARLES B. Photomicrography in Theory and Practice. New York (1944).

SINDALL, R. W. Paper Technology. London (1922).

SKINKLE, JOHN H. Textile Testing, Physical, Chemical and Microscopical. New York (1940).

SODERMAN AND O'CONNELL. *Modern Criminal Investigation.* New York (1935).

STEVENS, S. L. *Evidence of Arson.* Florida School for State Fire Marshals, Jacksonville (1945).

STILL, CHARLES E. *Styles in Crime.* New York (1938).

STRECKER, EDWARD A. *Fundamentals of Psychology.* Philadelphia (1945).

SUTHERLAND, E. H. *Principles of Criminology.* Chicago (1939).

TELLING, A. H. *The A, B, C of Plastering.* London (1927).

VOLLMER, AUGUST AND PARKER, ALFRED E. *Crime, Crooks and Cops.* New York (1937).

WILDER AND WENTWORTH. *Personal Identification.* Boston (1918).

WILLIS, A. M. *Smoke Marks and Their Meaning.* Florida School for State Fire Marshals, Jacksonville (1945).

WOOD, GEORGE. *Scientific Handwriting Testimony.* Boston (1918).

ZIMMERMAN, A. *Botanical Microtechnique.* New York (1893).